The T🛑lk
Curriculum

The Talk Curriculum

Edited by David Booth and Carol Thornley-Hall

HEINEMANN
Portsmouth, NH

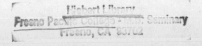

IN MEMORY OF ANDREW WILKINSON

© 1991 Pembroke Publishers Limited
528 Hood Road
Markham, Ontario
L3R 3K9

Published in the U.S.A. by
Heinemann Educational Books, Inc.
361 Hanover Street
Portsmouth, NH 03801-3959
ISBN (U.S.) 0-435-08597-2

Canadian Cataloguing in Publication Data

Main entry under title:

The Talk curriculum

Includes bibliographical references.
ISBN 0-921217-64-1

1. Oral communication.   2. Communication in education.   I. Booth, David W. (David Wallace), 1938-   . II. Thornley-Hall, Carol, 1936-

LB1572.T34 1991   371.1'022   C91-094041-X

Editor: David Kilgour
Design: John Zehethofer
Typesetting: Jay Tee Graphics Ltd.

Printed and bound in Canada
9 8 7 6 3 4 2 1

Contents

"Kidwatching" first appeared in *Observing the Language Learner* by Jaggar and Smith-Burke, IRA, 1985. Reprinted with the permission of Yetta Goodman and the International Reading Association.

"Learning to Teach by Uncovering Our Assumptions" first appeared in *Language Arts*, Vol. 64, No. 7. NCTE, 1987. Reprinted with the permission of Judith Newman and the National Council of Teachers of English.

"Bringing the Story to Life" first appeared in *Language Matters*, Vol. 283, Innter London Educational Authority, Centre for Language in Primary Education, 1988.

"Drama Talk" first appeared in *Drama Contact: The Journal for the Council of Drama in Education*, Vol. 12. Ontario, 1988.

We express our appreciation for their interest and support to the Ministry of Education for Ontario and the Peel Board of Education with special thanks to Iris Armstrong, George Badame, Bob Barton, Chris Bridge, Gen Ling Chang, Ron Cussona, Douglas Deller, Judith Fine, Brian Fleming, John Ford, Peter Guillemette, Dianna Hector, Wayne Hulley, Russ Jones, Ray Kaske, Sar Khan, Donna Kinch, Don Lawson, Lyn Mann, Debra Mitchell, Russell Moore, Wayne Moyle, Lynda Palazzi, Jo Phenix, David Pipe, John Rennie, Carolyn Rumley, Jane Sheills, Lynda Sutherland, Gordon Wells, John Wilcox, Andrew Wilkinson, Don Wood.

Introduction

Not too long ago a teacher's worth was measured by the silence in the classroom. The main mode of exchange was question and answer, and the students' extended talk time was composed of show and tell in Kindergarten and public speech in Grade 8. But things have changed. Today, schools are full of the sounds of children talking, and educators are examining the ways in which speaking and listening can be focused to maximize learning.

As we engage in talk, we literally tell the stories of our lives as we live them, constructing the realities of our beings through conversation. As individuals, we must somehow assimilate all our experiences and build them into our continuing picture of our world. The responses we get from our talk profoundly affect both the world picture we are creating and our view of ourselves. All talk, be it purposeful or random in nature, helps us understand the human race in all its variety, and is therefore an educational experience.

It is generally accepted in schools today that talk is a vital aspect of the learning curriculum. Language allows us to symbolize, structure, regulate, and give meaning to experience. As teachers, we must examine the nature of classroom talk, so that we can understand and harness its impact on the lives of children.

Generally, children in school have not been given time to hypothesize and talk themselves into understanding, to think out loud. Douglas Barnes called this groping towards meaning "exploratory talk", and it is usually marked by frequent hesitations, rephrasing, false starts, and changes in direction. This type of exploratory talk is one means by which the assimilation and accommodation of new knowledge to old is carried out. Talking can help children make sense "out loud" as they come to grips with new ideas. It is the bridge that helps them explore relationships that arise between what they know and what they are coming to know. If we can put our knowledge into words, then we begin to be able to reflect on that knowledge.

7

Children need opportunities to use language for a variety of purposes: planning, speculating, predicting, listening, organizing, storytelling, sequencing, interviewing, questioning, persuading, reporting, reasoning, criticizing, and evaluating. Joan Tough concluded that three factors are necessary in helping children reach their full language potential: dialogue with an empathetic adult; opportunities for imaginative play; and an enabling environment in which the child can encounter a variety of languaging experiences. Therefore, teachers have had to alter the communication patterns of the classroom, share the systems of interactive talk. They must negotiate the learning with the children, allowing them to express their thoughts and feelings within a social dynamic where the context rather than the teacher does the controlling. The teacher can be an actual listener, not an evaluator, and a whole new range of communication strategies can open up. We need context and purpose for talk, and the teacher must create situations that encourage talk within the limits of the classroom, with a maximum of individual expression and a minimum of thoughtless or self-indulgent behavior. Children express their ideas in search of reflection and refinement. When they are developing their speaking abilities, the responses of the listeners are an important indicator of whether they have successfully communicated their messages. We must help children extract new meanings from their experiences and communicate those meanings with coherent responses.

The writers contributing to this book all are committed to talk as a medium of learning in education. Their experiences and research with children demonstrate the value of speaking and listening within the context of authentic languaging events in the classroom. In each essay, the author describes and analyses one particular aspect of the talk curriculum, and relates that focus to the holistic nature of children engaged in learning: the necessity for a nurturing classroom environmnt; the intricate interrelationship of literacy and oracy; the need for observing the interactions of children in order to develop effective programs; the power of story as both a stimulus for talk and a means of structuring meaning; the role of drama in offering alternate contexts and voices for talk; the strength and support that networking and writing with other teachers provides; the effect that research in talk can have on program and practice, and the development of assessment strategies useful in promoting talk in the classroom.

Frank Smith reminds us of the need to avoid interfering in the natural progression of the education of children, and the talk curriculum requires this close scrutiny if we are to assist children in developing to the fullest their listening/speaking potential. We hope this book is a good starting point. It began with the TALK Project, an initiative of the Peel Board of Education and the Ontario Ministry of Education. The ideas of the authors who wrote these papers influenced many of the teachers who conducted studies in their own classrooms throughout the project. The teachers' own studies appear in a companion volume, *Classroom Talk*.

David Booth
Carol Thornley-Hall

Beginning Talk

William H. Moore has been a Supervisor of Language Arts for over thirty-five years. He pioneered the use of speech and drama in the schools of Ontario as a means of learning and as a way of developing communication strengths. As a speaker throughout North America, Bill Moore has informed and inspired teachers in their work with students of all ages, encouraging them to read aloud to their students and promoting techniques for involving students in the collaborative fabric of the classroom. His books include Words that Taste Good *and* Poems Please! *and his love of language and his passion for teaching have earned him respect with educators everywhere.*

In his article, "Some Thoughts on Talking with Children", Bill Moore outlines his philosophy for encouraging and enabling young people to want to participate in talk events in the classroom. His message is one of support, and his caring for children is evident in every strategy he suggests for both informal and formal modes of speaking and listening in the school setting.

Some Thoughts on Talking with Children

Language is what we teach, no matter what we teach, or, as
Marshall McLuhan put it: "The medium is the message."

Human beings differ from other primates principally in their
ability to communicate meaning, first in speech and later in
writing. Listening and speaking, reading and writing are what
we do when we communicate, and humans spend most of their
waking hours communicating with each other. That is why the
cruelest punishment is solitary confinement.

When children come to school they are placed in a strange
environment in which, most of the time, someone is talking
to them, and in which they are expected to listen for fairly
specific reasons.

Talking and listening are the most important skills we can
possibly teach our children, and yet these same skills are generally the most neglected. Somehow it is assumed that children
will pick up these skills by osmosis.

How do we talk to children? How do we get them to listen,
and, most importantly, to talk to us? We must accept the fact
that while most children have mastered most of the underlying structures of language by the time they reach school, the
way talk is *used* in school may be quite different from the home
experience.

At home conversation is generally one-on-one, often with a
loving adult. It tends to be free-ranging, and pretty well anything the child says is accepted. There are all kinds of delight-
ful digressions, and the child may interrupt more or less at will.
In school, discussion is relatively rare. In many classrooms,
most of the children seldom offer their opinions. The teacher's
opinion is often gospel, and the aim of the action is to reach
one specific point or conclusion. No longer may the child interrupt, but he or she must become accustomed to being part of
a large group. This is especially true for very young children
entering the primary grades. In many cases students learn very
early on that in school you keep your mouth shut, and listen
to the words of wisdom. Somehow we have to make sure that
this does not happen.

Let us look at some of the other problems young children may have to face when they start school.

The language of home is different from the language of school in many ways. Every family has its own private words for certain things. These words are the only words as far as the child is concerned, and so he or she uses them at school. For example, toilet words can be a particularly dangerous trap for a little child in school.

If a child is advanced in language development, he or she will use long words and difficult words quite naturally. Classmates may see this as showing off, and will take direct action against the bewildered speaker. On the other hand, a child may use odd pronunciations, personally developed phrases, and expressions, all of which are perfectly acceptable at home, but which cause laughter in school.

Sometimes the teacher's language is totally incomprehensible to the child. The teacher may use words the child has never heard before. Classrooms operate with a different vocabulary. The child may be confused. Also, many teachers tend to speak from a particular social status, while the child may come from a quite different background.

A child's language is one of the outward manifestations of personality and we have to do everything within our powers to make him or her feel that it is worthwhile, even though he or she may speak a different dialect and come from a home where respect for language is slight or non-existent. On the other hand, we fail children if we never attempt to bring them to the point at which they can use commonly accepted speech patterns. The trick is in finding ways to do this.

It begins with the atmosphere in the classroom. The authoritarian classroom will never do — the sort of place where the teacher is at the front dispensing nuggets of wisdom for the ignorant masses to swallow for later regurgitation. Equally hopeless is the room in which the children yell and scream at each other, and the teacher is reduced to a quivering wreck by the end of day one. Courtesy is essential at all times, and with this complete and utter trust. The children must trust the teacher, and the teacher must show the children in every word and action that they are looked upon as valuable and important human beings, with feelings that must be considered.

The formula is fairly simple: first the children must respect

13

the teacher. This means that the teacher must be prepared, knowledgeable, and fair. More than that, respect must develop for *everyone* in the classroom. Once this happens, learning can take place and talk can begin to flow.

All this may sound simplistic. Not at all. Teaching is not a science to be quantified and bottled. It is an art, and like all arts its essential core is emotional. Without an emotional bond between teacher and student, little true learning will occur.

Loving the teacher means having respect and affection, and knowing that the teacher will always be a safety net and never an executioner; realizing that the teacher will always listen and allow the child to share opinions. If there is trust, children will admit that they do not understand something. The admission of ignorance is the beginning of knowledge, but unless there is total trust no child is ever going to say, "I'm sorry, but I don't understand."

The essential first step in getting children to talk is to make them feel at ease. They must have enough confidence to feel free to make mistakes, to offer opinions, and to defend those opinions against the thoughts and ideas of others.

We develop this atmosphere from the start by listening carefully to what the children have to say, and making sure that every child has opportunities for participating. Courtesy is the grease that keeps the wheels of civilization turning, and stops them from squeaking too much.

We build children's confidence through constant approbation and support wherever possible. It may be that one of the deadliest sins of our world is the lack of warmth and commendation in our day-to-day activities.

We must create situations where children have opportunities to use language, to talk and to listen, to argue and agree. This means that we have to be willing to "waste" a certain amount of time. It may seem much more efficient to have the children copy a note from the board, memorize the facts, and recall them later, than to have an open-ended discussion about the matter, with the hope that some kind of conclusion will eventually be reached. I would argue that such time is not wasted at all. Within such discussions children have a chance to use language in many ways to get things done and keep the learning going. They use language to regulate behavior, their own and that of the rest of the group. They use language to maintain relationships within the group, a most important social activity. They use language to express their own special individuality. They use language to frame questions, the most powerful aid to learning. They gradually begin to free themselves to use language imaginatively. Above all, they discover that they are important individuals with ideas that are valuable.

We learn to talk by talking. We learn to listen by listening. The more we talk and listen to others talking, the better our ability to manipulate language. The better our ability to manipulate language, the better our ability to think and therefore to read and write, for both of these are thinking activities.

There are three main ways to work in a classroom: with the whole class, with small groups, and with individuals. All three have their place.

One of the best ways to begin is through storytelling. Here is the beginning of literature, and a comfortable, non-threatening way of stimulating talk. The story may be told by the teacher, then the children may work in pairs and tell the story to each other. Here they soon learn that every time the story is told the language may be slightly different, and that ideas can be expressed in many ways. Next, they can learn to interview each other, as characters in the story: after they have heard "The Three Little Pigs" and told it to each other, one child becomes the interviewing announcer while the other takes the part of one of the pigs. Interviews are a wonderful way of letting language loose. Most children have seen hundreds of interviews on television and know exactly how to conduct them. This same interviewing technique can be used through all the grades, with materials of ascending complexity. And the technique can be used in all subject areas.

Interviews are generally one-on-one, and the teacher can move unobtrusively about the room, dropping the odd hint here, adding the odd word there.

Most children are aware of the format of panels from television. The chairperson is usually the teacher at first. Gradually the teacher moves to the background and a child takes over. The chair organizes the operation, usually by asking certain questions, which various panel members answer. They should be encouraged to disagree with each other, for in this way children can air various points of view. The chair maintains order, and often summarizes at the end. Quite often, after an initial

15

period during which the panel alone are allowed to speak, the rest of the group is encouraged to participate. Once the format has been established, several panels can run at once in one classroom, with the teacher moving from one group to another.

Radio or television broadcasts can be made over the school P.A. system, with a daily news program or a series of interviews. They can also be done in the classroom. Tape recorders are invaluable here, for prerecording interviews and discussions. The writing and presenting of commercials is also a valuable activity. With the proliferation of hand-held camcorders in many schools, television programs can be put together by children for later broadcast. Once again, the whole class can be involved, possibly working in smaller groups.

Persuasive talk is a specialized kind of talk. Selling something demands certain very definite skills. Ads could be done live or on tape, audio, or video, and could sell imaginary products, school activities, books the children have just finished reading, or anything else of importance to them. This kind of talk might well begin as a whole class activity, and later be done in smaller groups.

Dramatization of all kinds is invaluable. Puppets, mime with narration, and storytelling can stimulate language activities and present children with all sorts of opportunities to use language orally.

In all these situations the teacher should be the catalyst, listening carefully, interjecting ideas from time to time, encouraging the shy to take part, making sure that certain children do not dominate. Listening to what children have to say is not always easy, with the multiplicity of demands upon the teacher, but it must be done. If you ignore what I am saying, you are telling me that I am of no importance whatsoever, and you are crushing my spirit. If you half-listen to me, and pretend that you are giving me your attention, you insult me and my ideas.

If we want to have a real and lasting impact in children's development we must somehow find time to give each one some individual attention on a regular basis. Working with individuals may well be the most valuable of all school activities. It is not easy to arrange, for with some thirty or more children in a class, the teacher's time is at a premium. But the minutes you spend with each child in personal, one-to-one talk may well be the one thing that child remembers years later, the one part of the week in which both you and the child learned immeasurably from each other.

We all need attention. We all crave attention. At the same time, at first we are not sure that we want to unburden our souls to some other person. This is where the student-teacher interview comes to the fore.

Organization is everything. We must arrange some way to schedule each interview, and this time must be inviolate. If I am to talk with you on Tuesday at a certain hour, then nothing must be allowed to interfere with our meeting. To begin with, about five minutes will be enough time. Such individual attention from a teacher every seven to ten days is greatly valuable to both teacher and student.

The physical set-up is important. We must avoid any confrontational arrangement in which the teacher sits behind an imposing desk, or on a higher level than the child. Try for a couple of chairs in a corner of the room, perhaps with a bit of carpet, and a slight screen to separate the talkers from the rest of the class. The situation must be easy and relaxed. For many children this may be the very first time in school that they have ever had an adult's undivided attention, and many of them may be uneasy.

At the first encounter, be prepared for some stiffness on the part of both teacher and child. It is often a good idea to open with some fairly general points. Every child has some area of expertise, something he or she knows more about than most others. As teachers we must be aware of these pockets of knowledge and interest, and we can often start by talking about them. Avoid questions that appear to be loaded, like, "Did you like that story I read today?" This puts any child in a most uncomfortable position. Rather, try to keep all your questions as open-ended as possible, so that the child has manoeuvring room. Sometimes it pays to chat about school activities, a model the child has made, and so on. As children get used to such teacher-pupil talks, they will often open up about all manner of things, and you will learn much about their feelings and fears, motivations and problems. At the same time, they will realize that you are truly interested in their ideas.

To get the ball rolling you can chat about hobbies, games, favorite television programs, family, all the things important to the children's lives outside school. If what they say is accepted, you make them feel important. Constant support and interest in what they have to say are essential, as is the way you throw in ideas of your own, linking their experiences with yours. If there is anything they have found trouble with in any subject area, here is the place to talk it through. Pictures they have drawn and painted, journals they have written, poems and stories they have read or created can all be talked about in this special sharing time.

Once children get used to this personal five or eight minutes with their teacher, they enjoy it thoroughly, and the major problem becomes that of limiting the talk to just a brief time.

If the children have been involved in an individualized reading program, the books may become the focus of the talks. If such a program does not exist, then a story you are reading to the class, something they have done in a "reader", a poem or story the class has enjoyed together can be the basis for discussion.

This time you and each child spend together might be called a teacher-student conference. I prefer the term teacher-student interview, because that is what happens: you interview each other. At first the teacher initiates the questions, but gradually the student starts taking over. The storytelling and interviewing suggested earlier will have given the children plenty of opportunities to hone their interviewing skills. If you study good interviewers on television or radio you will note that they draw out their partners, and let them do most of the talking. This is the aim here as well.

After many months of such experiences children might even begin interviewing each other, following the pattern you have established. This is useful, but will never replace the power of several minutes of uninterrupted talk alone with the teacher.

All this will not happen at once. There will be disasters along the way. These can be turned into valuable lessons if you discuss them with the children, and try to find out why things went wrong. Given a chance to talk over such "failures", children can be most perceptive.

Once children become accustomed to this kind of discussion you can begin to be quite demanding. No longer will you accept statements like, "I think the hero is stupid when he does so and so." Now you will say, "Ah, yes. And why do you say that?

Show me some lines from the story that support what you have just said." Later, when the children trust you utterly, you might even say, "I think you are quite wrong there. Try to counter these arguments. . . ." and then present them with a series of differing ideas. Don't do this at first, or the children will dry up, possibly for good!

The degree of sophistication in these interviews will increase by leaps and bounds. Interestingly, primary children have far less trouble with such situations than older children, who have become more self-conscious and afraid.

In a school where talking with children is accepted as important to their development, the children will begin to feel secure in what they say, and will trust themselves. They will start understanding why they answer the way they do, and thus begin to know who they are. They will start respecting the opinions and ideas of others, while at the same time learning to differentiate between the true and the spurious. They will realize that not everybody always agrees with them and that such behavior is quite acceptable in our society.

If we admit that all children are important, listen to them with respect, and talk to them with consideration, then they will develop not only in language ability but in every other way.

Observing Talk

Yetta M. Goodman is a professor of education at the University of Arizona, where, with her husband Ken, she has been the driving force behind the whole language movement in North America. She is the author of many significant writings on language and education, and has developed the theory of miscue analysis for assessing the reading progress of children. In her seminars and workshops, Yetta Goodman has promoted the use of authentic literacy events as the foundation of language growth and development, where students in a school setting are engaged in actual languaging activities, reading books by real authors, writing as real writers, and talking about issues and events that have significance to them.

In this seminal article on "kidwatching", Yetta Goodman outlines her philosophy of assessing children's progress in order to develop effective programs of instruction. She encourages teachers to observe the children in classroom activities, to find ways of extending reading and writing activities, to help children reflect on their own thinking, to lead them to do what they cannot do themselves, and to trust in children's learning — and their own.

Kidwatching: Observing Children in the Classroom

YETTA M. GOODMAN

Three first-graders were grouped around the flotation bowl. They were trying to discover what things could float and why. Elana put a wadded piece of foil in the bowl. Just as it sank to the bottom, Mr. Borton walked up and observed the scene. He noticed a wet, fair sized aluminum boat next to the bowl.

He addressed the group, "What did you just learn?"

Elana responded quickly, "Big things float and small things sink."

Robin reacted, "Uh, uh. I don't think that's always true."

"What might you do to prove the hypothesis Elana just made?" said Borton.

"Well," said Lynn, "maybe we could make a small boat and a big ball and try those things to see what will happen." As the children got involved in the new tasks they set for themselves, Borton walked on to another group.

Good teachers, like Mr. Borton, have always been kidwatchers. The concept of kidwatching is not new. It grows out of the child study movement that reached a peak in the 1930s, providing a great deal of knowledge about human growth and development. Teachers can translate child study into its most universal form: learning about children by watching how they learn. The term kidwatching has caught on among those who believe that children learn language best in an environment rich with opportunities to explore interesting objects and ideas. Through observing the reading, writing, speaking, and listening of friendly, interactive peers, interested, kidwatching teachers can understand and support child language development.

Evaluation of the progress of conceptual and language development for individual children cannot be provided in any useful sense by formalized pencil and paper tests. Evaluation provides the most significant information if it occurs continuously and simultaneously with the experiences in which the learning is taking place. Borton knows a lot about how children conceptualize, develop new insights into the physical nature of the world, and what kinds of language they use and have developed during the activity in which they were involved.

22

Even in the home, parents are aware of how much their children have grown, whether they have become better ball players or how much more considerate they have become toward other family members. Parents know this by their constant attention to and involvement with size of clothes, the faster and harder return of a pitched ball, or some deed a child does for a parent or sibling. Scales and yardsticks may provide some statistical data for parents to use to verify their observational knowledge, but it is never a lone measure on which they rely.

Unfortunately, especially in recent years, scores on tests have been viewed as more objective than the judgment of a professional observer since test results are often presented under an aura of statistical "significance" which for many people has an unquestionable mystique.

Formal tests, standardized or criterion-referenced, provide statistical measures of the product of learning but only as supplementary evidence for professional judgments about the growth of children. If teachers rely on formalized tests they come to conclusions about children's growth based on data from a single source. Tests do provide evidence of how children grow in their ability to handle test situations but not in their ability to handle settings where important language learning occurs. Studies of the role that context plays in how children learn have made it clear that children respond differently in different situations. Teachers who observe the development of language and knowledge in children in different settings become aware of important milestones in children's development that tests cannot reveal.

Kidwatching, the focus of this paper, is used as a slogan to reinstate and legitimatize the significance of professional observation in the classroom. Those who support such child study understand that the evaluation of pupils' growth and curriculum development are integrally related. The energies of teachers and other curriculum planners must go into building a powerful learning environment. The key question in evaluation is not, "Can the child perform the specific tasks that have been taught?" Rather, the question is, "Can the child adjust language used in other situations to meet the demands of new settings?" The teacher must be aware that children learn all the time. The best way to gain insight into language learning is to observe children using language to explore all kinds of concepts in art, social studies, math, science, or physical education.

Teachers screen their observations through their philosophy, their knowledge base, and their assumptions whenever they are involved in kidwatching. Following are some of the basic premises that underlie kidwatching notions:

1. Current knowledge about child language and conceptual development must be a part of continuous education for teachers. Such knowledge guides observations. Not only does it help teachers know what to look for as signs of growth and development but it also helps teachers become consciously aware of their knowledge, their biases, and their philosophical orientation.

2. Language and concepts grow and develop depending on the settings in which they occur, the experiences that children have in those settings, and the interaction of the people in those settings. The richer and more varied these settings and interactions, the richer the child's language and concepts will be.

3. Knowledgeable teachers ready to assume responsibility for observation and evaluation of children play a very significant role in enriching each child's development of language and concepts.

Current Knowledge about Language

During the second half of this century a knowledge explosion has occurred in the study of language or linguistics. Much of this knowledge is contrary to the ideas about language which have been taught in the past under the labels of phonics, spelling, vocabulary, and grammar. In addition, there have been enormous gains in understandings about how children learn language. When old beliefs are being questioned and new knowledge is not fully understood, a great deal of controversy is often generated. This is especially true of those who have to apply the knowledge, as teachers do in classroom situations.

There are many issues concerning language differences in the areas of both dialect and second language learning which teachers must consider. Too many children have been hurt in the past because of lack of knowledge about language differences. Not only teachers but test makers and curriculum builders often produce materials that reflect myths and misunderstandings. The more knowledge teachers have about language variation, the better position they are in to evaluate materials and tests in order to use them wisely and appropriately. Attitudes such as "these children have no language" or "bilingualism confuses children" are still too prevalent. Kidwatching can help teachers be aware of how such statements are damaging to language growth, if they are armed with up-to-date knowledge. By observing the language of children in a wide variety of settings such as role playing, retelling of picture books, or playing games during recess or physical education, teachers gain many kinds of information that help to dispel myths about language and language learning.

For example, Sorita, age six, would use the following types of construction often in oral conversations with other children or during sharing sessions:

"Lots of my friends was at my house. . . ."
"We was going to the store. . . ."

However, during her narration of "The Three Billy Goats Gruff" which accompanied the acting out of the story by some of her classmates, her teacher heard, "There were three billy goats. . . ." Sorita used this more formal construction throughout the narration.

Retelling a story, about a farmer and his son, a recent nine-year-old immigrant from Lebanon said, "They were working at to plant something."

Both examples provide insight into each child's language development. Sorita shows the ability to use the more formal "were" form in storytelling although she uses the colloquial form in the informal settings. She is aware of formal and informal language settings and that each permits different language.

The second child shows growing control over two kinds of complex English structures — the verb plus particle "working at" and the infinitive form "to plant," even though as this child combines the structures, they may sound a little unusual to a native English speaker's ear.

Errors in language and in conceptual development reflect much more than a mistake that can be eradicated with a red pencil or a verbal admonition. What an adult perceives as wrong

25

may in actuality reflect development in the child. Errors, miscues, or misconceptions usually indicate ways in which a child is organizing the world at that moment. As children develop conceptually and linguistically, their errors shift from those that represent unsophisticated conclusions to ones that show greater sophistication. The previous examples are evidence of this kind of growth. Sometimes teachers expect certain responses or "correct answers" because of a school-based cultural view of the world. The child's unexpected responses, if observed with understanding, may broaden a teacher's conceptualization about the child's world. "Errors" also indicate interpretations which may in no way be wrong but simply show that the child has used inferences about reading or listening which were unexpected.

For example, a kindergarten teacher gave her class a short talk about what was wrong with wasting milk prior to morning snack time. Tomasa was observed taking a small sip of milk. She then carefully closed the milk carton, wiped her place with her paper towel, and slowly placed the carton of milk in the waste basket, holding it tight until it reached the bottom.

"Didn't we just talk about not wasting milk?" Miss Dasson asked.

"I ain't waste my milk," Tomasa responded. "I keeped everything real clean!"

Miss Dasson now knows that "waste" has an alternate meaning in the language of Tomasa's community — "to spill." She and Tomasa can now share each other's meanings.

The kidwatcher who understands the role of unexpected responses will use children's errors and miscues to chart their growth and development and to understand the personal and cultural history of the child. There are no tests available which can provide this kind of data to the professional educator. These insights can emerge only from kidwatching based on a sound knowledge of language and language learning.

Individual teachers may not be in a position to keep current about the dynamic information so vital to understanding language learning. However, courses of study or programs can be organized through setting up teacher support groups, working cooperatively with teacher educators at local universities and colleges or with in-service personnel at the district level, and holding discussion groups. Although courses in linguistics, the science of language, may in themselves be helpful, it may be more useful if teachers encourage and participate in the development of programs which have an applied orientation for the classroom.

Variations of Setting, Function, and Material

Thoughtful observation of children takes place in a rich, innovative curriculum in the hands of a knowledgeable teacher who demands and accepts responsibility for curriculum decision making. With such teachers, children are involved in exciting educational experiences and make the greatest growth in language learning and conceptual development.

Curriculum becomes sterilized when it is based on pupils' results on standardized tests or progress on "criterion-referenced" behavioral checksheets. In order to achieve appropriate gains, curriculum experiences must narrow to those safely entombed in the test itself. Curriculum becomes repetitive practice with the same kind of "skills" on workbooks and worksheets as in the test. The only individualization is how much practice each pupil must endure.

Where kidwatching is an integral part of the curriculum, the teacher's focus is on providing rich learning experiences for children. There is an awareness of the dynamic relationship among the teacher, the children, and the experiences. Evaluation is ongoing. Although teachers should certainly be expected to document and discuss the growth of their children, the most important role of the teacher is involving children in learning through the richness of the curriculum. Only when children have a variety of materials available to read and many good personal reasons to want to learn about new ideas and concepts will they read various genres, write for different purposes, and grow in their ability to use written language effectively.

As functions and purposes for learning new concepts change, so will the settings, the language, and the materials needed for the learning. These broadened experiences enrich language learning for children and provide many opportunities for kidwatching to occur. Children must go to the library to solve certain problems, to the principal's office to solve others. They interview some people orally, read about others, or write letters as it serves the purposes of their explorations. Language learning reaches out to meet new challenges and teachers can evaluate the flexibility with which children can expand language use.

For example, keeping copies of children's letters written to different people over the course of a few months provides evidence about: 1) the appropriateness of the language of the letters, depending on their purposes; 2) the degree to which children change the language and style of the letters, depending on their audience; 3) the increase of conventionally spelled words over time; 4) changes in the complexity of grammatical structures; and 5) concern for legibility.

Teacher's Role Is Significant

Concepts from three scholars in different fields of child study provide a jumping off place from which to explore the significance of the teacher's role. Jerome Bruner talks about "scaffolding"; M.A.K. Halliday about "tracking"; and L.S. Vygotsky about the "zone of proximal development". Each of these concepts is used to express the significance of communicative interactions between adults and children which are basic to the expansion of language and the extension of learning in children. If parents play as significant a role in a child's language development as these scholars suggest, it seems logical that a teacher with understandings about how children learn language might capitalize on their ideas and be even more effective than parents in supporting child language growth and extending it once the child comes to school.

Focusing on mother/child interaction, Bruner (1978) defines scaffolding by quoting Roger Brown:

> A study of detailed mother/child interaction . . . shows that successful communication on one level is always the launching platform for attempts at communication on a more adult level. . . .
> The mother systematically changes her BT (Baby Talk) in order to "raise the ante" or alter the conditions she imposes on the child's speech in different settings.

According to Bruner, the adult always takes the child's ideas seriously, thinking through what the child is trying to communicate, allowing the child to move ahead when capable of doing so, and supporting the child only when the child seems to need help.

28

Once the child has made a step forward, she [the mother] will not let him slide back. She assures that he go on with the next construction to develop a next platform for his next launch.

Halliday (1982) uses a similar notion about language learning in children, which he calls tracking. From his extensive study of language development, Halliday concludes that the adults and older siblings who live with a child "share in the language-creating process along with the child". He suggests that teachers take on a similar role when the child comes to school, helping children find new ways to say or write things as children find new reasons to express themselves or to understand.

Vygotsky (1962), who adds additional perspectives on the significance of child/adult interaction, believes that educators can make use of cooperation between adult and student and "lead the child to what he could not yet do" by himself.

Vygotsky defines the "discrepancy between a child's actual mental age and the level he reaches in solving problems with assistance" as the child's zone of proximal development.

> With assistance every child can do more than he can by himself. . . . What the child can do in cooperation today, he can do alone tomorrow. Therefore, the only kind of instruction is that which marches ahead of development and leads it, it must be aimed not so much at the ripe as at the ripening functions.

Although there may be some theoretical differences among these scholars, there is little disagreement about the significance of the role of the teacher or other adults involved in children's growth. Teachers who continually observe children using knowledge about language and cognition can ask the appropriate question, or pose a specific problem, or place an object in front of children so that learning is extended. As they observe, they also gain information for planning new experiences or instructional activities, leading the child toward new explorations. Observation, evaluation, and curriculum planning go hand-in-hand.

Teachers can develop a variety of ways to keep records of these developments for reporting to parents, to remind themselves of children's growth over the year, to involve students in self-evaluation, and to leave records for continued school use. However, the records of kidwatchers are not simply statistics used to compare children or to have them compete with one another. Whether they are anecdotal records of children's interactions; selected writing samples of students' letters, logs, and stories; or tapes of children's reading or oral reporting, their purpose is to provide profiles of the children's language growth in different settings, with different materials, and through different experiences.

Where to Start? What to Do?

My own observations of outstanding kidwatching teachers are reflected in the following suggestions:

1. When a child achieves success in some communicative setting (including reading and writing), the teacher may find a number of ways to extend this to a new and different setting. For example, a child who is responding orally to a patterned language book such as *I Know an Old Woman Who Swallowed a Fly* can be encouraged to write a book entitled *Johnny Swallowed a Bumblebee*, either alone, with the teacher, or with a peer. This would extend the holistically remembered oral reading of a book to writing a book to share with others using similar language structures but personalizing characters and experiences in writing. But don't expect the new use of communication to look as successful as the one previously achieved. When a child tries something new it is bound to seem less sophisticated at first than something the child does which is familiar.

2. When children are involved in exploratory activities, the teacher might raise questions such as "I wonder why this is so?" or "What do you think is happening here?" The questions may help children reflect on their own thinking and see contradictions in their hypotheses.

3. When children are observed to be troubled with an experience, the teacher can move in and talk about the situation with them and lead them to what they cannot yet do by themselves (Vygotsky, 1962). It is at a moment of frustration that a kidwatching teacher can help children resolve conflictive situations à la Piaget (1977) and move on to expand their language and conceptualization.

4. Teachers need to trust in children's learning and in their own ability to learn along with their children. Language learning involves risk taking. When teachers believe in their own professional judgment and respect the children's ability, success occurs as part of the curricular experiences. With such a sense of security teachers can become kidwatchers and with the children build a community which contains many launching pads from which the children and the teacher can reach the next level of language learning together.

Story Talk

Bob Barton is an educational consultant with a deep and wide-ranging background in education. As a classroom teacher, consultant, and education officer for the Ontario Ministry of Education, and lecturer in two faculties of education, Bob Barton has promoted storytelling as a strategy for bringing the best in literature to children, and for providing young people with a means of responding to the stories they listen to and read. His books Tell Me Another *and* Stories in the Classroom *have given teachers strength as story users in their classrooms, and his speeches and workshops on storytelling have encouraged teachers throughout North America to explore the art of storytelling in the classroom.*

In the following article, Bob Barton describes his beliefs in storytelling and his strategies for assisting teachers in working with the power of story. His interests lie in helping children and teachers discover the "heart of the tale", so that they can breathe their own lives into the author's story, causing the words of others to become their own. When teachers share stories they are doing what storytellers have done throughout the ages.

Bringing the Story to Life

BOB BARTON

At the ninth annual Toronto Storytelling Festival last February, Duncan Williamson, a guest storyteller from Scotland, remarked that when he told a story he was ever mindful of the person who had passed it on to him.

Other storytellers have made similar comments when discussing their art. Those who have grown up with or are familiar with the oral tradition are often as aware of the teller of the tale and the way the story was told as they are of the story itself.

Diane Wolkstein gives this description of a Haitian storyteller in *The Magic Orange Tree*:

> Dadi told this story in front of her house in Carrefour-Dufort. The full moon shone behind her as she described the flight of the birds (Pee O lay) in the sky. She stood on tiptoes and her arms formed circles above her head, each arm rotating outward from the centre of her body. As the intensity of the story increased, her circles became smaller and faster. When the birds turned and turned she used her right arm only and very quickly rotated it in front of her chest in a clockwise motion, with a bent elbow. She spoke the words "turn and turn and turn" in one breath and stopped when her breath gave out. It was a very dramatic and touching storytelling.

Many of us were read to at home but haven't retained vivid memories of the performance.

Others who grew up with radio recall fondly the voice mannerisms of favorite radio personalities, and can recreate the performance of early commercials. Occasionally a pattern of sound or turn of phrase from early memories of someone close to us enters our conversations.

For most of us who find our stories in books, however, the big challenge will be how to bring the story to life. Anyone can find a story, learn the plot, and tell it. But that doesn't necessarily make for memorable storytelling. To be memorable, the story must be invested with the thoughts and feelings of the teller. When we imitate, we fail.

Teachers have a great advantage where storytelling is concerned, for the children we work with comprise a wonderfully supportive community of listeners and tellers. When we make that community central to our work with stories, endless opportunities present themselves for exploring ways to bring life to the work on the page.

By creating a community open to exploring stories adventurously the teacher can easily bring stories, lots of them, to life in the classroom. At the same time, the skills of storytelling can be practised and polished. Among the approaches available to us are communal enactment, communal composing, communal interpretation, and communal wondering.

Communal Enactment

Probably the most common form of communal enactment in schools comprises singing songs such as "The Farmer in the Dell", "Old Roger", "The Grand Old Duke of York", and many modern examples from the school playground such as:

Jack mac
Rim ram rac
Re rio ro
And a bobtail black
Say. . .

The simple movement patterns (circling, advancing, retreating, passing under arches) of these enactments are easily transferable to countless other little narratives from the oral tradition. I marvel at the genius of the Ahlbergs (*Each Peach Pear Plum*, *The Jolly Postman*) as they pluck from nursery rhymes, nursery stories, and children's folklore, characters, events, patterns of speech, and singing rhythms, and construct new frameworks which combine these ingredients. Similar opportunities await us if we dip into the same sources and employ the ritual patterns of oral storytelling which are characteristic of the singing and drama games of street and playground.

Using a circle formation and simple movement pattern of advancing to the centre and retreating, what might be the possibilities for chanting together:

If all the seas were one sea
What a great sea that would be.

If all the trees were one tree
What a great tree that would be.

35

If all beings were one being
What a great being that would be.

If all the axes were one axe
What a great axe that would be.

And if the great being took the great axe
and chopped down the great tree.

And if the great tree fell into the great sea
What a great SPLASH that would be!

Using a series of tableaux developed cumulatively, how might the bright images of sun, wind, and sky take shape in enacting:

White bird featherless
Flew from Paradise
Pitched on the castle wall;
Along came Lord Landless
Took it up Handless
And rode away horseless
to the King's white hall.

With older children, the Opies' *Children's Games in Street and Playground* have sparked some wonderful story enactments. *King of the Barbarees* (sung to the tune of "Hang Down Your Head, Tom Dooley" and restructured as a mime play) is an exellent example.

There is a King, Queen, Princess, Captain of the Guard, and some soldiers, also a Castle which consists of two children holding hands. The King tells the Captain of the Guard to march round the Castle singing.
  "Will you surrender, will you surrender,
  The King of the Barbarees?"
The Castle replies,
  "We won't surrender, we won't surrender,
  The King of the Barbarees."
Captain,
  "I'll tell the King, I'll tell the King.
  The King of the Barbarees."
Castle,
  "You can tell the King, you can tell the King,
  The King of the Barbarees."
The Captain goes back to the King and, stamping his foot, says,
  "They won't surrender, they won't surrender,
  The King of the Barbarees."

36

The King says, "Take two of my trusty soldiers."
The soldiers follow the Captain and the rhyme is repeated again.
   "Will you surrender, will you surrender,
   The King of the Barbarees?"
This goes on until all the soldiers have joined the ring, then the
King says, "Take my daughter." Next to go is the Queen, and
last of all the King. The King says, "We'll break down your
gates," and after the rhyme has been said again with the King
joining in, everybody makes a line with the King in front. He
takes a run and jumps on the hands that are linked together and
tries to break through them, while the two who are at the Castle
count to ten. If he does not break through, he goes back and one
of the soldiers has a turn. They all jump on the Castle, one at
a time, and try to break it down. If they do not succeed the Castle
has won.

Enactments need not be physical. Simple stories found in
traditional folk songs can be chanted in call-and-response
fashion. Singing choruses blended with the spoken word can
result in some very powerful communal storytelling. From
Geoffrey Summerfield's *Junior Voices 2, Didn't It Rain*, aug-
menting by a two-part singing chorus — side A singing, "It ain't
gonna rain no more, no more", etc. and side B singing, "It's rain-
ing, it's pouring, the old man is snoring" at the top of the piece
and at the end — makes this song sermon a rousing event.

   Didn't it rain

Now, didn't it rain, children
God's gonna 'stroy this world with water,
Now didn't it rain, my Lord,
Now didn't it, rain, rain, rain.

Well, it rained forty days and it rained forty nights,
There wasn't no land nowhere in sight,
God sent a raven to carry the news,
He histe his wings and away he flew.

Well, it rained forty days and forty nights without stopping,
Noah was glad when the rain stopped a-dropping
God sent Noah a rainbow sign,
Says, "No more water, but fire next time."

They knocked at the window and they knocked at the door,
They cried, "O Noah, please take me on board."
Noah cried, "You're full of sin,
The Lord's got the key and you can't get in."

37

Traditional American

Charles Causley's *Early in the Morning* contains some terrific new material for communal enactment. *Nicholas Naylor* chanted and accompanied with a sea shanty became an instant favorite in one classroom.

Nicholas Naylor

Nicholas Naylor
The deep-blue sailor
Sailed the sea
As a master-tailor.

He sewed for the Captain,
He sewed for the crew,
He sewed up the kit-bags
And Hammocks too.

He sewed up a serpent,
He sewed up a shark,
He sewed up a sailor
In a Bag of dark.

How do you like
Your work, master-tailor?
"So, so, so."
Said Nicholas Naylor.

Longer tales from the oral tradition or contemporary stories modeled on patterns from the oral tradition are suitable also.

There is a story by Linda Williams, *The Little Old Lady Who Wasn't Afraid of Anything*, which is extremely enjoyable. The plot is simple. A little old lady goes into the woods to collect nuts and berries and seeds. She stays too late and is overtaken by night. As she rushes along the path home she encounters a pair of clomping boots, wriggling trousers, a flapping shirt, two white gloves, a tall black hat, and eventually a large, scary jack-o-lantern. All chase the old woman to her house where she barricades herself behind locked doors. However, she is the little old lady who isn't afraid of anything, isn't she? The story can't end this way. How she handles her dilemma is both clever and funny.

Because the story is repetitive and cumulative and supports prediction, the telling of it invites much chiming in. For example, each meeting ("Right in the middle of the path were two big shoes") is followed by a description of the noise that the object makes: "And the shoes went, CLOMP, CLOMP."

Each time the old woman flees from the object, the words, "But behind her she could hear. . ." are repeated.

Ever so slight a pause each time the teller approaches these bits of the story never fails to elicit the vocal prediction of the listeners.

As the children get caught up in the mystery, fun, and chiming in with known bits, confidence grows and the story, borne on the playful and imaginative interchange between teller and audience, comes to life magnificently.

Many stories both traditional and contemporary readily yield their sounds, shapes, and secrets when explored in this fashion by teachers and their classes.

Communal Composition

Communal composition — composing pieces together spontaneously — resembles rapping in many ways. The object of the activity is to improvise with words, rhythms, and sounds using a single theme or subject.

The theme or subject is discussed in terms of what information the group knows about it. This material is sorted, classified, and ordered into an "out loud" experience. For example, a composition on how words play might result in an inventory of all the ways this occurs (palindromes, puns, etc.), and examples of these in action; a framework of unison choruses, antiphonal choruses, solos, and songs is then developed.

From a class composition entitled "Flummery" (words at play) comes this bit:

Chorus in unison chants: Palindromes, palindromes
Solo:　　　　　　　　　 Left to right
Chorus:　　　　　　　　 Madam I'm Adam
Solo:　　　　　　　　　 Right to left
Chorus:　　　　　　　　 Madam I'm Adam

One teacher capitalized on her class's interest in proverbs. She introduced to her children John Agard's *Say it Again Granny*, a collection of twenty poems based on Caribbean proverbs. It became the source for the following group composition.

39

All:	Granny says [chanted three times with sharp rhythmic clapping "dada-da-dada" interspersed between the words]
Group A [unison]	Early to bed and early to rise Makes one healthy, wealthy, and wise
Group B [unison]	That's what Granny says!
Group B [unison]	Birds of a feather flock together
Group A [unison]	That's what Granny says!
Group B [unison singing]	Mother may I go out to swim?
Group A [unison singing]	Yes, darling granddaughter. Hang your clothes on a hickory stick but don't go near the water.
Group B [unison chanting under solos]	Granny always tells you
Solo A	A stitch in time saves nine
Solo B	Don't count your chickens before they hatch
Solo C	Still waters run deep

The ending of the piece was played as a game. The children were divided into groups and given a proverb to disguise by "padding" it. For example the proverb "a watched pot never boils" might become "a vessel containing H_2O seldom reaches 212°F. when scrutinized constantly."

Each group in turn chanted its "padded proverb", while the rest of the class tried to echo the actual one.

Communal Interpretation

Vi Hilbert, Skagit Elder of the Salish people, is recognized throughout America as a storyteller, researcher, and teacher of the language and traditions of the Lushootseed-speaking people of the Northwest. Vi points out that how people play with their voices is central to storytelling among the native peoples of North America.

Play with the voice, exploring the possibilities for the voice, is the focus of communal interpretation. Together and in small groups, the class reads aloud, endeavoring to capture the voice of the storyteller by answering the question, "Who is telling this story to whom and why?"

40

Narrative poetry, from nursery rhymes to contemporary verse, makes an excellent source for group oral reading. Poet Judith Nicholls' "Moses . . . a sequence", in *Magic Mirror*, became an exciting challenge for one class. Before introducing the poem, the teacher read from the Old Testament the story of Moses and the exodus from Egypt. She asked the children to be aware of any five things that made a pattern. At the conclusion of the reading the children made lists of patterns they had discovered. For example, some made lists of magical transformations (e.g., burning bush, staff to serpent, water to blood), others made lists of water imagery. The children were then asked to explain the "big idea" behind their patterns.

Using an overhead projector, the teacher introduced the five poems which comprise "Moses . . . a sequence". After the children had opportunities to read the poems silently and out loud, they attempted to figure out the big idea behind Nicholls's pattern. They settled on groups of speakers, each telling an aspect of the Moses story from unique points of view. To test their idea each poem was assigned to a group whose task was to bring to life the voice of the speaker, and to convey in the oral reading both intended audience and purpose for telling the story.

Here is the first poem in the sequence:

Searcher

Princess, what are you dreaming
   down among the moist rushes?

Soft pleated linen, beaded bracelets,
   purple grapes and Pharaoh's finest wines
   await you at the palace —
   yet you follow
   a wavering baby's cry.

The group working with this poem decided that the voice was that of ladies-in-waiting, gossiping among themselves in the bulrushes as they observed Pharaoh's daughter following the cries of the baby Moses. Hushed voices and mocking tones were employed to put this across.

Interpretations of the other pieces ranged from work songs of laborers told in call-and-response fashion and games played by children, to a cast rehearsal of a play celebrating the crossing of the Red Sea by descendants of the Israelites.

For these children, the saga of Israel became just that! By

41

approaching text in this way these children were discovering that storytelling is as much about how the story is shaped as it is about what happened to whom and why.

Communal Wondering

Communal wondering encourages children to discover that the heart of storytelling lies in the ability to project oneself imaginatively into the story and to determine what is important about the story for oneself. To accomplish this, children are encouraged to retell the story in a variety of ways, to question the story, and to explore possible answers within the "Story Community".

One group of twelve-year-olds read a story about a fisherman who discovered a selchie woman, stole her seal skin, forced her to marry him, and eventually lost her to the sea again.

In their efforts to retell that story, the children:

1. divided the story into scenes and briefly sketched each scene cartoon strip fashion;
2. in small groups developed a list of questions they would like to ask about the story;
3. in small groups developed a list of questions they would like to ask about the story;
4. chose their most important question and came together as a class to explain why their question was important in understanding the story;
5. as a class chose one of the questions to pursue further (in this case the question was, "Why, after she grew to love her family on land, did she give them up the instant she found her skin?");
6. role-played a village meeting with the selchie woman at which time the villagers attempted to test all the superstitions they held about selchies;
7. in small groups, round-robin fashion, retold the story in the first person as the selchie woman;
8. examined three retellings of this story by Susan Cooper, Mordecai Gerstein, and Helen Waddell respectively and discussed the retelling that spoke most powerfully to them.

For these children storytelling became so much more than finding a story, memorizing it, and giving it back orally word for word. The more they talked about it, thought about it, revisited it, the more they became aware of the incredible power and energy that stories possess.

It is important to foster openness to stories and to avoid activities which seek to regulate and control them. Talking about the images we see, the musical sounds we hear, and our ideas of what we think the story is telling us should be central to our work with storytelling in the classroom. If this is so, the problems of bringing the story to life will turn into a real adventure. At the same time, our memories of the stories we have worked with will have been enriched by the involvement of our community of classroom storytellers.

Book Talk

*Gordon Wells is well known for his work on language develop-
ment and the role of language in education. Currently, he is
a professor of education at the Ontario Institute for Studies
in Education in Toronto. For fifteen years Gordon Wells was
the director of the longitudinal study "Language at Home and
at School" in Bristol, England, and he is continuing his studies
of language and learning by working collaboratively with
teachers, both in his graduate courses and for various school
boards, to explore ways of improving opportunities for language
development. Professor Wells was instrumental in designing
the project on TALK for the Peel Board of Education, and
travels widely, giving lectures and workshops emphasizing the
importance of quality interaction with children.*

*In his paper "Talk about Text: Where Literacy is Learned
and Taught", Gordon Wells examines the ways in which
learners engage with print, and offers suggestions as to the role
of the teacher in creating classroom communities where collaborative talk about texts can empower children in becoming literate, thinking individuals.*

Talk About Text: Where Literacy is Learned and Taught

GORDON WELLS

My aim in this paper is to offer an account of literacy and its development and to explore the role that talk about texts plays in that development. I want also to set talk about texts within a Vygotskian perspective of learning as "assisted performance" (Tharp and Gallimore, 1989). And, finally, I want to say something about teachers learning how to promote the development of literacy through the inquiries that they carry out in their own classrooms and about the role that talks about texts of a different kind plays in their learning.*

Let me start with a discussion of literacy and, more specifically, with a sketch of the historical development of written language.

Literacy: A Technology for the Empowerment of Mind

Of course, we cannot be sure what the origins of written language were but, almost certainly, writing was used very early as a form of external memory for information of practical importance. For example, in order to preserve them for future use, oil, wine, corn, and so on, would be stored in sealed clay vessels. Initially, someone would have to remember what was in the different jars or, in the absence of such a person, the jars would have to be opened at random in order to discover what was inside. Marking a symbol on the outside of the pot relieved this burden on memory — provided that the symbols used could be interpreted according to some shared conventions. Similarly,

* Earlier versions of this paper were presented as a seminar in the Eminent Scholar series at the Martha L. King Center for Language and Literacy, Ohio State University, June 1989, and at the First International Conference on Language and Learning, Kuala Lumpur, July 1989. The classroom research on which it is partly based was carried out under grants received from the Ontario Ministry of Education, the Toronto Board of Education, and the Ontario Institute for Studies in Education. However, the views here expressed are those of the author and not necessarily those of the funding agencies.

I should like to express my gratitude to Gen Ling Chang for the collaborative thinking, writing, and talking over several years out of which this paper has grown. I have also benefited from the helpful comments of David Olson, Magdelene Lampert, and Michael Cole in revising earlier drafts.

written symbols were used to record taxes paid or owing, or to list valuable possessions. For similar reasons of this kind, a number of civilizations independently invented ways of giving systematic visual representation to linguistic meanings — based on morphemes, syllables, or phonemes. But, whatever the basis of the relationship between linguistic meaning and visual symbol, the crucial feature that all these systems had in common was that, in contrast to speech, they allowed meaning to be preserved beyond the point of utterance. That is to say, for the first time, they enabled meaning to be represented in a medium that was permanent — or at least relatively so.

Once the significance of this characteristic of the written text had been grasped, the use of the new technology expanded into other areas. And as the range of uses expanded, so did the techniques and conventions of representation. To the principle of alphabetization, first found in a complete form in the Greek script, were gradually added constant left-to-right directionality, spacing between words, paragraphing, pagination, tables of contents, indexes, and so on, all of which greatly increased the ability of the written text to function as a free-standing representation of meaning, independent of the intentions in the mind of the writer at the time of writing and of the particular context in which it was produced or to which it originally referred (Morrison, 1987).

It was this context-independent permanence of written texts that made the invention of writing such an important cultural achievement. For, in addition to the capturing of information of a purely practical kind, it made possible the preservation and accumulation of discursive information on a wide variety of topics far beyond what a single individual could discover and remember for him or herself. Thus, by exploiting this "archival" function of writing (Olson, 1977) — by systematically collating, comparing, and organizing the texts produced by others — scholars over time gradually established the textual basis of the subject disciplines that we know today. Indeed, it is no exaggeration to say that, without some form of permanent, external, conventional system for representing meaning, the achievements of modern science and technology would be inconceivable, as would serious study in any of the humanistic disciplines. (For thorough discussions of the historical development of literacy in western societies and of its conse-

47

quences for ways of thinking, see Goody, 1977, and Ong, 1982).

But the sheer accumulation of information does not, in itself, lead to knowledge. For knowledge, being a state of understanding achieved through constructive mental effort, requires the individual to engage with the relevant texts in a critical and creative manner in an attempt to bring about a correspondence between the meaning represented in the text and the meaning represented in the mind (Flower, 1987; Wells et al. in press). And it is this latter function of written language — as a medium through which individuals, through the interrogation of their own or others' texts, can extend their own thinking and understanding — that led Bruner, speaking at a recent conference on orality and literacy, to characterize literacy as "a technology for the empowerment of mind".

A Model of Literacy: Text Types and Modes of Engagement

The foregoing history of written language is, of course, incomplete: for example, I have neglected to say anything about the social aspects of literacy — its function in creating communities of like-minded thinkers and the role it has played in the development of such institutions as religion and the law (Stock, 1983). My intention, however, has been to emphasize certain intellectual functions that written language has gradually come to perform in order to propose a more general model of literacy in contemporary society, based on a distinction between different modes of engaging with written texts.

Every written text has a physical form — marks inscribed on a surface which represent the writer's meanings according to the conventions of a linguistic code. When the user of a text focuses on the code — on the encoding/decoding relationship between meaning and its physical representation, and the conventions which govern it — I shall talk about this as engaging with the text in the *performative* mode. This is the mode we adopt, for example, when we are proofreading something we have written or when we are skimming through a telephone directory, looking for a particular entry. Of necessity, beginning readers and writers have to devote a considerable amount of their attention to learning how to use the code. However, even for them, a concern with form is rarely the primary

48

purpose. Competence in the performative mode is therefore best seen as a means to engaging with the text in other modes; as long as that competence is adequate for the purpose at hand, it functions below the level of conscious attention.

The second mode of engagement that I wish to distinguish has its origins in the very first uses of written language. This I shall call the *functional* mode. In this mode, we treat the text as an adjunct or means to the achievement of some other purpose as, for example, when using the appropriate form to put money in the bank, consulting a timetable to plan a journey, leaving instructions for another family member on what to prepare for dinner, or finding out from an instruction manual how to use a recently acquired machine. In these contexts, we engage with the various texts in order to act, and the texts function as means to that end.

The third mode of engagement I shall call the *informational*. In this mode we treat the text as a channel by means of which information is communicated from one person to another; the validity or significance of the information being communicated is not at issue, rather the focus is on accuracy of comprehension or on clarity and conciseness of expression. Consulting a reference book to find out facts related to a question or to identify an unknown flower or bird would be examples of this mode of engagement, as would writing a routine report or completing a questionnaire.

In the fourth mode, by contrast, the text is engaged with as a verbal artifact. In calling this mode the *re-creational*, I intend to capture the sense of engagement with the text being an end in itself, undertaken for the pleasure of constructing and exploring a world through words, one's own or those of another author. Whilst much of our reading of imaginative literature is undertaken in this mode, other genres can be read in the same way; this is also likely to be the mode in which we write 'expressively' (Britton et al., 1975), for example, letters to friends or entries in a personal journal.

Important though each of these modes of engagement is in the course of everyday life, however, none fully exploits the potential of written text as this was described at the end of the previous section. For that we need to introduce a fifth mode of engagement, which I shall call the *epistemic*. It is in this mode that the text is treated, not as a representation of meaning that is already decided, given, and self-evident, but rather as a tentative and provisional attempt on the part of the writer to capture his or her current understanding in an external form so that it may provoke further attempts at understanding as the writer or some other reader interrogates the text in order to interpret its meaning.

When one reads what someone else has written in order to try to understand what it can mean; when one considers alternative possible interpretation and looks for internal evidence to choose between them; when one asks, "Is the text internally consistent?" and, "Does it make sense in relation to my own experience?" one is engaging with the text epistemically. Similarly, one reads a text that one is writing oneself. However, there is an important difference between reading and writing in terms of the contribution that each makes to the construction of knowledge. In the course of reading one may see connections between things one already knows or achieve insights of feeling and understanding that go beyond the already known. Unfortunately, however, the mental representations created through reading fade almost as quickly as those created in the course of oral communication and even rereading provides no guarantee of recapturing them.

It is here that writing is so powerful. For, by writing them down, those insights and perceived connections can be captured so that they can be returned to, critically examined, reconsidered, and perhaps made the basis for the construction of a further sustained text of one's own. And in the creation of one's own text one is forced to go even further in the development of one's understanding; for, at all stages in its creation, one is involved in a variety of constructive mental processes: assessing what one knows about the topic and what one does not know that one needs to come to know; selecting what is relevant from this knowledge for the purpose in hand; and organizing and expressing it in the form most appropriate to achieve this purpose with respect to the intended audience. Sustained writing on any topic of importance to the writer thus involves a fruitful dialectic between what Scardamalia and Bereiter (1985) refer to as "the content space and the rhetorical space". Furthermore, since each attempt to resolve that dialectic through the construction of a particular text leaves a record in the form of a working draft, one can return to the draft as one's own first critical reader to discover what it means and then work to revise it and, through both processes, extend one's understanding of the topic about which one is writing (Murray, 1982).

This, then, is the empowerment that comes from engaging with texts epistemically: as reader or writer (and particularly as writer), by conducting the transaction between the representation on the page and the representation in the head, one can make intellectual advances that would otherwise be impossible to achieve. To be *fully* literate, therefore, is to have both the ability and the disposition to engage with texts epistemically when the occasion demands.

Although they can be seen as of differential significance for the intellectual development of individuals and of the societies of which they are members, the five modes of engaging with texts that I have just outlined should be thought of as complementary with respect to the range of purposes that written languge serves, rather than as mutually exclusive. Moreover, it is important to emphasize that any text can be engaged within any of the five modes, and that, during a complete literacy event, one may move between modes, with each mode supporting and facilitating the others. Indeed, I have just argued that any sustained piece of writing will almost necessarily involve an epistemic mode of engagement and this will demand engagement in one or more of the other modes at appropriate points for its full achievement.

Nevertheless, there is a strong tendency for texts of any particular type to elicit a dominant mode of engagement — particularly in the case of reading — by virtue of the function that that text is designed to serve in the lives of those who engage with it. Reference books, for example, are most commonly read to obtain information, TV guides consulted to organize viewing, cheques written to pay bills, and so on. The extent and quality of a person's literacy will thus be strongly influenced by the types of text that he or she most frequently encounters as reader or writer, since this will tend to determine which modes of engagement are most frequently practised.

This being so, it is worth pausing for a moment to consider the types of written text that students most frequently encounter in school. For the relative emphasis that is given to different types of text and to the purposes for which students are expected to engage with them must surely be important in shaping the concepts of the nature and value of literacy that they construct.

Reading and Writing Texts in the Classroom

For the purposes of argument, let me propose a rather crude four-way classification of the types of text that are found in abundance in almost all schools as a starting-point for such an investigation.* First, the basal reading series, with all its associated exercises and worksheets, the prime purpose of which is to instruct the student in the use of the conventions of the written code (Heap, 1985). Second, the notices displayed at various points around the school, instructing visitors to report to the office, students not to run in the corridors, and so on. In individual classrooms are to be found texts of the same basic type concerning the feeding of classroom pets, due dates and times for the completion of work, and so on. The third category consists of the textbooks that are the basic resource for the teaching of most subjects in the curriculum; into this category also fall the reference books of various kinds that are used as supplementary material. The final category, by contrast, is much more heterogeneous and is to be found in the school or classroom library and in the desks, cupboards, and tote-bags of individual students. What characterizes the texts in this category is that, by and large, they were written, not by a committee with the deliberate intention of shaping people's beliefs and behaviors, but by individual authors who cared enough about their topics to want, through words, to create worlds to be explored, delighted in, and reflected upon.

From the growing number of observational studies in classrooms, we can predict with some confidence the pattern of relationships that is likely to hold between these four categories of text and the five modes of engagement that I outlined earlier.

* Considerable effort has been devoted to the attempt to produce a taxonomy of text-types, starting with the classical rhetoricians and continuing to the present day. In recent years, notable contributions have been made by Britton et al. (1975) in their study of secondary students' writing, and by Halliday and his associates at the University of Sydney in the field of genre study. However, because such attempts have been motivated by different purposes, they have given rise to a number of alternative taxonomies, none of which is exhaustive or of universal applicability.

The basal reading series, being predominantly concerned with providing instruction in the skills involved in reading and writing, tends to emphasize the performative mode of engagement, with a secondary emphasis on the informational. Although the stories and poems that such readers contain could be engaged with re-creationally and epistemically, actual observation suggests that this rarely occurs; instead, the emphasis is, first, on accurately reading the text aloud and then on correctly answering factual questions by locating the information in the text or by drawing culturally warranted inferences from related real-world knowledge (Heap, 1985). The second category of texts, being concerned with regulating action, tends to elicit a functional mode of engagement. Interestingly, although it is "functional literacy" (or illiteracy) which is at the forefront of concern about falling standards in schools, such action-oriented texts, and the associated functional mode of engagement, are rarely given explicit attention in school; it is presumably assumed that, being so ubiquitous, they are unproblematic.

For text and reference books, the dominant mode of engagement tends to be the informational. Such instructional texts, being designed in general to transmit the culturally sanctioned facts and values of a given subject area in an orderly and predetermined sequence, assume — or are ascribed — an authority which militates against the questioning and critical stance which characterizes the epistemic mode of engagement (Olson, 1980; Luke, de Castell, and Luke, 1983). To a considerable extent, the same emphasis on an informational mode of engagement characterizes the students' written assignments that are based on the study of instructional texts (Britton et al., 1975). Produced to demonstrate adequate and accurate absorption of the required information, such student texts show little tendency to speculate, to question the established view, or to offer alternative perspectives.

For the category of what might be called "real" books, it is difficult to say with confidence what mode of engagement they elicit. If their authors were consulted, they would no doubt say that their intention was to engage their readers re-creationally and, hopefully, also epistemically. However, when novels and other works of literature are selected for class study, they are all too often subverted for purposes similar to those that typify the use of the basal reader, with an emphasis on literal comprehension and the drawing of inferences predetermined by the teacher (Baker and Freebody, 1989). Similarly, students' own extended writing of an imaginative or discursive kind is, by the way in which it is responded to by the teacher, reduced to an occasion for attention to spelling, punctuation, and the avoidance of stylistic solecisms.

Where, then, do students have the opportunity to engage with texts in a re-creational or epistemic mode within the prescribed curriculum? The answer is that, in many classrooms, there is no such opportunity. Of course, this does not mean that students do not engage in re-creational reading and, to a lesser extent, writing, but only in the few minutes before recess when they have finished the "real" work, or in their own time outside the classroom. On occasion, too, when their own purposes demand it, they may adopt an epistemic mode of engagement. But as the direct focus of teacher and student concern, classrooms in which a re-creational mode of engagement with texts is deliberately planned are rare, and those in which the epistemic mode is given systematic attention are even rarer.

Exactly where the relative emphasis falls obviously varies from teacher to teacher. But there is sufficient evidence from classroom research to suggest that, despite the impressive statements of aims to be found in policy statements, the transmission-oriented curriculum that actually operates in many classrooms — and at all levels of education — has the effect of constraining both the range of text-types that are given explicit attention and the opportunities to engage with texts of any type in ways which encourage those characteristics of critical and constructive thinking which I have called epistemic.

Some will no doubt reply that epistemic literacy is indeed the goal towards which they are striving but that it is premature to attempt to get students to engage with texts in that mode until they have mastered prerequisite skills and accumulated necessary information. In effect, what they are proposing is another version of the pedagogical fallacy which equates the developmental sequence of learning with the abstract hierarchy of skills which is used to organize instruction. However, just as in learning to talk, children do not first learn lexical items and the syntactic structures in which to combine them, and only then use these linguistic resources to interact with other people and to learn about the world, so too, in learning to be literate, they do not need to have fully mastered the code and the information contained in the text in order to begin to interact with it epistemically. Indeed, just the reverse. For it is when children understand, from shared story-reading, that texts are representations of worlds waiting to be explored, challenged, and even improved upon, that they will be most strongly motivated to master the performative mode of engagement so that they can read them for themselves (Wells, 1986). Similarly, when students in school are encouraged to treat texts, not as authoritative pronouncements, but as contributions to an ongoing discourse in which they can be active participants in the search for understanding, they will be more inclined to acquire the range of skills and strategies that are necessary for this participation. In sum, since the epistemic mode of engagement with texts subsumes all the other modes, it should be seen, not as a distant and unattainable goal, but as the most effective point of entry for literacy learning and as the focus for each unit of work at every level of education. For if students are to discover the potential that literacy has to empower their thinking, feeling, and action — in other words, to become fully literate — they must engage with texts in this way at all stages in their development.

How this can be achieved will be the burden of the latter half of this paper. But first I want to extend our definition of "text".

Texts as Symbolic Representations

What is important about a text, I suggested earlier, is that it is an external and permanent linguistic representation of the meanings intended by its producer. But, if that is so, there are surely other modes in which these objectives can be achieved, for example in algebraic equations or in scientific formulae. There is no problem in treating these as texts, for in each case they are representations couched in a conventional language. What about a diagram, a flow chart, or a musical score? Here too, there seems to be no difficulty in extending the notion of text to cover them as, in each case, they employ an explicit and conventional symbolic system. But what about a painting or a model? These must be more controversial, since although they are symbolic representations, the conventions in terms of which they are created are much less explicit. Nevertheless,

55

I want to suggest that it is heuristically worthwhile to extend the notion of text to any artifact that is constructed as a representation of meaning using a conventional symbolic system since, by virtue of its permanence and the symbolic mode in which it is created, such an artifact performs the essential function of allowing us to create an external, fixed representation of the sense we make of our experience so that we may reflect upon and manipulate it.

Having come this far, it is only a small step to recognizing the existence of another class of potential texts, which are around us all the time in the form of oral discourse. With the invention of the tape recorder, it has become possible to capture episodes of talk in a permanent form so that they too can be reheard and reviewed in very much the same way as written texts. Of course, the practice of recording important speech events in writing has a long history, for example in the law court record or in notes taken in lectures. But it is only the advent of the tape recorder that has made it possible to capture verbatim the utterances actually spoken.

However, even before the invention of electronic recording devices — or even of writing — there were ways of making speech memorable so that it achieved a sort of permanence which made it potentially available for reflection. The most obvious examples are the great oral epics, such as Homer's *Iliad*, which were clearly texts in the sense in which I defined the term, and, no doubt, on occasion they elicited the sort of engagement that we should recognize as epistemic.

But there is little doubt that it was as a result of the growing pervasiveness of written texts in all aspects of life that the literate practice of distinguishing the form of the message — the text — from the intentions of its producer were carried over to the spoken mode of communication so that, when the occasion demands, literate people can give the same sort of critical attention to oral texts as they habitually give to texts in the written mode. And it is probably this practice, as much as the shared engagement with written texts, that provides the introduction to literacy for those children who grow up in highly literate homes.

In a recent discussion of pre-school experiences which prepare children for the literacy demands of school, Heath (1986) has developed this idea by identifying a number of such "oral literacy events", that is to say events in which what is said is made the focus of attention. One of the categories that she discusses is the "recount", which is the sort of text that might be produced when a small child and one parent have returned from a visit to the park or the local supermarket and the accompanying parent asks the child to tell the other parent about the visit. Under such conditions, the child's recounting of what happened is likely to be closely monitored for its accuracy and completeness and, where necessary, corrected or extended, with the result that the child is, in effect, invited to monitor his or her oral rendition in very much the same way as one might treat the draft of a written text.

Other oral events that invite the same attention to the form as well as the content of what is said can be found in the "show-and-tell" time that is a common event in the primary grades, or in the academic lecture or the contributions to a debate. What I want to suggest, therefore, is that, with or without the aid of a tape recorder, there is quite a wide variety of occasions on which close attention is given to the actual words spoken, as well as to the speaker's intentions, so that it is appropriate to extend the notion of text to include such oral productions within its scope.

So, having arrived at a working definition of texts, we can use this and the notion of different modes of engagement with texts to attempt a tentative and provisional characterization of what it is to be literate. *To be literate is to have the disposition to engage appropriately with texts of different types in order to empower action, thinking, and feeling in the context of purposeful social activity.*

Literacy Learning as a Cultural Apprenticeship

To define literacy in dispositional terms is to emphasize the use of the relevant skills, as well as their possession. And it is a similar emphasis on learning through meaningful use which lies behind Smith's (1983) characterization of learning to read and write as joining the literacy club. Youngsters, he suggests, learn to read by reading, and to write by writing, in the company of fully paid-up club members, whose own behavior provides demonstrations both of what is worth doing and of how to do it. Another way of putting this is to say that becoming literate

57

is best seen in terms of an apprenticeship, in which the learner is inducted into the model of literacy implicitly held by the more expert performer. And in an earlier paper (1987), I showed how differences in success in literacy learning in school, which are found in a wide variety of cultures, could be accounted for by the socially based differences in the value given to different types of text and modes of engaging with them that learners encounter in their communities as well as in their classrooms.

Learning through apprenticeship is, in fact, a universal phenomenon and is the normal mode through which most cultural practices are acquired. Described by Rogoff and colleagues (forthcoming) as "guided participation in situations of joint involvement with other people in culturally important activities", it is what Vygotsky (1978) had in mind in his well-known exposition of "learning in the zone of proximal development". In his view, all cultural knowledge and, indeed, the higher mental processes themselves are acquired through social interaction as, in the course of shared participation in a joint activity, the more mature member of the culture, whilst enacting the total process, draws the novice into participation and gradually allows him or her to take over more and more of the task, as he or she shows the ability to do so.

In many of the instances of cultural learning that have so far been studied, it is clear that it is from demonstration and hands-on performance that the child gradually appropriates the relevant behavior (i.e., learns why and how to perform the constituent actions). However these forms of collaboration are most appropriate for cultural practices of a predominantly physical kind, such as kneading dough, tieing shoelaces, or weaving on a handloom (Rogoff, in press). In the case of less predominantly physical activities such as reading or writing, they seem less likely to be sufficient. Indeed, since these literate practices are, as we have just seen, essentially a matter of engaging with a particular text in a manner appropriate to one's goals on a particular occasion, it is difficult to see how such essentially *mental* abilities could be acquired by simply observing an expert's overt behavior. Equally, it is of little value to guide the novice's action if he or she has no understanding of the significance of the action to the overall goal of the activity. What this means, therefore, is that in the case of such cultural practices as those associated with literacy, talk in and about the activity can no longer remain an optional aspect of the collaboration, as in the case of such practices as weaving or baking, but must be seen as both central and essential.

Consider, as an example, such a familiar shared literacy practice as a parent and child choosing grocery items from the shelves on a shopping expedition to the local supermarket. In this context, the adult's silent reading of the labels on the packets would not be transparently meaningful (nor probably even observable) to a youngster who did not know that the symbols on the outside of the packets corresponded to the contents on the inside and that the differences between the configurations of symbols were systematically and conventionally related to differences between the spoken words that are used to differentially label the contents. In practice, of course, adults who want their children to learn from this shared activity not only read the labels aloud but also verbally draw attention to the salient symbols on the labels and the nature of the contents; they probably also offer explanations of what they are doing.

It is for this reason that, although I agree with Smith on the importance he attaches to children learning to read and write by reading and writing real texts for purposes that are personally meaningful to them, I want to emphasize the importance of their participation in *joint* literacy events in which the significance of the literate behavior is *made overt through talk*. It is in such verbally mediated assisted performance — in talk about text — that literacy is learned and taught.

In the next section of this paper, therefore, a number of examples of talk about text will be examined in an attempt to discover precisely what kinds of opportunities for becoming literate they provide. First we shall consider some typical literacy events observed in the home; then we shall look at some examples of talk about text in the classroom.

Talk about Text at Home and at School

The first example, which is taken from Tizard and Hughes's (1984) study of four-year-old girls at home and at nursery school, concerns the revision of a shopping list. Pauline's mother is crossing off her list the items that her neighbor has just offered to bring back for her from the local store. Pauline, on the other hand, has a further item that she wants to add to the list.

Mother: We've only got that little bit of shopping to get now [shows Pauline the list].

Child: Mummy? Can I have one of them drinks? Can I?

Mother: Get some more drink?

Child: Yeah. Can write it down on there [points to where she wants it written on the list]. Up here.

Mother: I'll get you some when I go tomorrow.

Child: Aw! [disappointed]

Mother: All right? 'Cause I'm not getting it today.

Child: No . . . In, in the Vivo's? [the local store]

Mother: Haven't got Daddy's money yet.

[For several turns they discuss the need to have enough money to pay for all the items]

Child: Mum, let's have a look! [Mother shows child the list] Do it again.

Mother: We gotta get rice, tea, braising steak, cheese, pickle, carrots, fish, chicken, bread, eggs, bacon, beefburgers, beans . . . Oh, Irene's gone to get them [crosses off beans] . . . peas, ham, corned beef.

Child: And what's that? [points to a word on the list]

Mother: That's lemon drink [crosses off 'lemon drink'] She's just gone down to get that one. See?

Commenting on this episode, Tizard and Hughes write, "a shopping list provides an extremely vivid demonstration of the way in which written language may be used within a meaningful human activity. The power of the written word lies in its ability to link up different contexts in space or time, and here it is doing precisely that — forming a link between the home, where the decisions and choices are made, and the shop, where they are carried out". And it is precisely because of its embeddedness in the routines of everyday life that this episode is so effective in pointing up this link. For not only are the items that are included in the list meaningful in terms of Pauline's knowledge of the ingredients used in the preparation of meals and snacks, but she is also made aware of the practical constraints on the inclusion of items: "Haven't got Daddy's money yet". At the same time, she is allowed to participate in the construction of the list by requesting an item for inclusion, but with her mother doing the actual writing in the place that Pauline has designated.

Put in terms of the broad categories introduced earlier, this event clearly involves an action-oriented text; equally clear, the dominant mode of engagement with the text is functional. And it is the specific functional connection between text and action — the relationship between the structure and the content of this list and the particular objects and actions in the practical world to which it is related — that is pointed up in the talk in which the items to be included are negotiated. This is what is made available for learning here and Pauline shows that she has indeed achieved some grasp of the function of the text when she asks her mother to add a drink for her to the list. But, as in most literacy events, the functional is not the only mode of engagement which is called into play. When Pauline's mother writes on the list, and again when Pauline asks about a particular word on the list, it is the performative mode that is brought into focus. Through close attention to specific entries in the list, matching the visual display with the encoded meaning, she is also meeting the evidence which, over many such occasions, will allow her to construct a representation of the written code itself and of how to use it. As in most naturally occurring literacy events, however, the performative mode of engagement remains instrumental: the actual acts of reading and writing are means to the achievement of a larger purpose.

My second example comes from a study of shared book reading by Sulzby and Teale (1987). In this episode, Hanna (age 2.2) and her mother are reading a label book called *Baby Animals*.

Mother: [reading] "Kittens are baby cats."
Hannah: Tha- . . . that's the mommy cat?
Mother: The mommy is the cat; the babies are kittens. Can you
    say kittens?
Hannah: Kittens.
Mother: That's right. Kittens.
Hannah: It's . . . up here. (pointing to the back and tail of a kit-
    ten that can be seen over the back of the basket in the
    picture)
Mother: Is that . . . that's the back end of a baby kitten, isn't it?
    And there's his ear sticking up. See? Is that his ear?
Hannah: [nods]
Mother: What's he playing in?
Hannah: In yarn.
Mother: Is he playing in the yarn basket?
Hannah: Yes. See? [laughing]

Here we have a composite text, consisting of pictures and brief statements that label or comment on the pictures. Not surprisingly, given Hannah's age, it is the pictures which occupy most of her attention. But, as can be seen in this brief extract, the two modalities of the composite text work together, the words cueing the way in which the pictures should be understood, and the pictures providing referents for the words. And this is how the mother enacts the event with Hannah, first explaining the definitional statement through expansion and then, in response to Hannah's observation, going on to discuss some of the details of the representation of the kitten.

In terms of the different text-types distinguished above, this would seem to be an instructional text, its purpose being to teach the linguistically appropriate way of categorizing objects in the world. As might be expected, therefore, the mode in which mother and child engage with the text is predominantly informational. At the same time, there is also a concern on the mother's part to ensure that Hannah can engage with the text performatively in the sense of being able to "read" the picture.

My third example involves a somewhat older child in a study I worked on in 1986. David (age three) has chosen a picture story book called *The Giant Jam Sandwich*, which he has had read to him several times before. In the story, a swarm of wasps descends on the town of Itching Down and the inhabitants try, by various means, to get rid of the attacking horde.

Mother: [reads] "They drove the picknickers away,
    They chased the farmers from their hay.
    They stung Lord Swell on his fat bald--;;
David: Pate
Mother: D'you know what a pate is?
David: What?
Mother: What d'you think it is?
David: Hair.
Mother: Well — yes. It's where his hair *should* be. It's his head
    — look, his bald head. All his hair's gone.
David: Where is it?
Mother: Well, he's old, so it's dropped out. He's gone bald.

After a little more of the text has been read, David's attention is taken by a picture in which three male inhabitants of Itching Down can be seen, each trying in his own way to fight off the wasps.

David: Is that a spray to shoo them away?

Mother: Yes. It's probably some sort of insecticide . . . to get rid of them. And what's that net for, do you think? [a butterfly net]

David: It's for catching them with.

Mother: It doesn't seem to be much good though, does it?

David: No. They come out the holes.

Mother: [laughs] The holes are too big, aren't they? And what about this man? What's he got?

David: He's — What's he got? [The man is wielding a fly swatter]

Mother: What's that?

David: A note. What does the note say?

Mother: A note on a stick, is it? Is that what you think?

David: Actually it's a sound.

Mother: A what?

David: A sound. What's it called on the stick? What is it? What's that man got?

Mother: Well you know — um —

David: Yes . . . Sign.

Mother: You think it's a sign? Yes it looks very *like* a sign with writing on, doesn't it?

David: Yes.

Mother: But it isn't. It's like Mummy's um — fish slice [slotted spatula].

David: What is it?

Mother: It's a swatter. He's going to hit the wasp with it.

In its combination of words and pictures, this composite text has certain similarities with the one that Hannah and her mother were reading. However, there are two important differences. First, the words here form a sustained text which is self-contextualizing; although they certainly complement the written text and add an extra dimension of detail to it, the pictures are not necessary for its interpretation. Secondly, the purpose of this text is not to instruct but to delight; words and pictures together create an imaginary world which the reader is invited to enter and explore. In terms of the different text-types, then, this is an example of literature — a "real" book.

To describe the dominant mode of engagement that is enacted here, by contrast, is much more difficult. In the course of the whole event from which these two episodes have been extracted, David and his mother engage with the text from a variety of points of view. David's first response is affective, as he expresses his dislike of wasps; later he is concerned about the harm they might cause. In the first episode quoted here, there is also evidence of an informational mode of engagement, as David completes the line of verse with the word "pate", and his mother goes on to explore and extend his understanding of its meaning. In the second episode, it is David's "reading" of the picture that is at issue; he appears to think that the man is holding a written sign telling the wasps to go away. His mother helps him to clarify this interpretation over several turns, expressing appreciation of its plausibility, before finally offering her own, adult interpretation. To characterize this as an instance of epistemic engagement may be to make too strong a claim. However, in the talk in which they savour and explore the imaginary world created through the words and pictures, David is being helped to construct and evaluate alternative interpretations in a way that is at least incipiently epistemic as well as very clearly re-creational.

In presenting these three examples, it is the differences between them that I have so far tended to emphasize. And these are important. For although in none of them is the text engaged with in only one mode, there is a strong tendency for a particular mode to dominate according to the type of text involved. This was Sulzby and Teale's conclusion too, based on a much more systematic sampling of shared storybook readings: even within this much narrower range of text-types, they found that "characteristic patterns of reading interaction [were] associated with different types of text" (1987). If children are to be introduced to the full potential of literacy, therefore, it is important that they should participate in a wide range of literacy events so that they meet texts of different types and learn how to engage with them appropriately. However, if, as I have suggested, it is the epistemic mode of engagement that most fully exploits the potential of texts for the empowerment of thinking, opportunities should be found for shared literacy events in which the texts involved are likely to elicit this mode of engagement. In the pre-school years, it seems, this is most likely to occur in the context of shared storybook reading.

The three examples also share some important similarities, however. For, despite the differences in the type of text involved, in each of them the talk between mother and child enacts appropriate ways of engaging with the particular text, thus providing an opportunity for learning about how to engage with a text of that type. In each case, too, the child is encouraged to be an active participant in the event and has his or her contributions as composer or interpreter of the text validated by the adult's acceptance and support. How important these features are can be seen more clearly when they are compared with those that characterize the events that form the staple of the literacy curriculum at school.

Consider the following episode from a session in which the teacher is reading to a group of five-year-olds. The picture storybook, *Little Black Sambo*, has been read without interruptions. The extract below (Wells, 1985) is taken from the talk which immediately follows the reading.

T: What did the first tiger take off Little Black Sambo?
P1: Shirt.
[T does not respond]
P2: His coat.
T: His coat that his mummy had made. Do you remember when his mummy made it — what colour was it?
Ps: Red.
T: Red, yes . . . What did the second tiger take?
Ps: Trousers.
T: His trousers. . . What did the third tiger take?
Ps: Shoes.
T: Was he pleased to take the shoes?
Ps: Yes.
Ps: No.
T: Why not?
P1: Because he had forty feet.
T: He said — what did he say to him?
P2: I've got four feet and you've. . .
T: I've got four feet and you've got —?
Ps: Two.
T: You haven't got enough shoes for me.

After more talk of the same kind, the children moved on to another activity.

There are two points that I want to make about this episode by way of contrast with the three preceding examples. The first concerns the impoverished model of literacy that is enacted in the limited — and limiting — question-and-answer sequence, which is the only mode in which the teacher draws the children into engaging with the text. Even the "why" question that the teacher asks is not a genuine request for an inference on

65

the children's part, as the reason for the third tiger's dissatisfaction with the shoes is given in the text itself. Thus, by treating the text solely as a series of items of information to be correctly recalled, the teacher reduces this picture storybook to an instructional text, thereby excluding any possibility of the sort of affective and exploratory talk which was so central a feature of David and his mother's discussion of the book they were reading. Secondly, and as a direct consequence, there is no sense of collaboration. The children dutifully conform to the teacher's agenda but, given no opportunity to express their own reactions to the story, they provide no evidence on the basis of which the teacher could assess the growing edge of their understanding and work with them to extend it through "guided participation".

Unfortunately, such instances of missed opportunities are all too common in school. Indeed, according to some observers, the testing of "factual" comprehension constitutes the dominant mode of talk about text, whatever the type of text that is being read (Durkin, 1979). Nor, in many cases, are the texts children themselves produce used as an opportunity for collaborative talk that extends their grasp of either the content or the medium of expression. Unlike the home examples discussed above, the talk that occurs tends to be confined to just two modes — the informational, and the performative that is needed to support it.

Some would argue that it is the conditions of the classroom that constrain what can be achieved: the externally imposed requirement on teachers to "cover the curriculum" in the limited time available, which leads to their unwillingness to allow time for the serious consideration of students' points of view, or the perceived impossibility of responding individually to the number of students for whom they are responsible. Others see the problem to be in the students themselves: their backgrounds and previous experience, it is thought, have not equipped them to be active, independent constructors of meaning who can, with guidance and support, engage with texts in the epistemic mode. This view is often linked to a conviction that students will only be capable of literate thinking when, having been instructed in a predetermined sequence of skill-building exercises, they have mastered all the prerequisite component skills. Whatever the reason, however, the fact of the matter is that in a high proportion of classrooms, at all grade levels, texts are rarely treated as an invitation to discuss alternative possibilities of interpretation or expression, and so students have little opportunity to discover, through such collaborative talk, how an epistemic engagement with text can be a powerful means of achieving understanding.

There are teachers, however, who have discovered that there are viable alternatives to a transmission-oriented curriculum. Trusting in their students' disposition actively to make sense of their experience, and reconceptualizing the teaching-learning relationship in terms of transaction rather than transmission, they have found that much more can be achieved in their classrooms than they would originally have believed possible. In the following section, I will present examples taken from the work of two such teachers to illustrate a variety of collaborative activities in which talk about texts provides a much wider range of opportunities for learning to be literate. These examples are taken from observations made in the course of a longitudinal study carried out in four downtown elementary schools serving multilingual communities in Toronto.*

Preparing a Group Presentation

The following episode is taken from a unit of work carried out in Helen Whaley's Grade Six classroom in which the students, working in groups organized in terms of reading level, have been studying novels. As the culmination of the unit, each group is to make a presentation to the rest of the class that will give their peers some appreciation of the novel they have read. The form of presentation is a matter for each group to decide, the only constraint being that it should involve both oral and written modes of language use. In practice, most groups have decided to include: a dramatization of an episode from the novel, written texts that might have been written by characters in the

* The project, entitled "Language and Learning: Effecting Change through Collaborative Research in Multilingual Schools", involved a collaborative exploration of the provision and uptake of learning opportunities in classrooms in which the majority of students were from ethnolinguistic minority backgrounds. The children chosen for longitudinal observation were initially selected at three different grade levels (Senior Kindergarten, Grade Two, and Grade Four), and from four different ethnolinguistic backgrounds (Chinese-, Greek-, Portuguese-, and English-speaking) and were studied for a period of three years (Wells et al. forthcoming).

novel, a collage of illustrations with explanatory written text, and some form of oral commentary. The following extracts are taken from a complete morning session during which the groups were reviewing their material in preparation for the final presentations.

The session started with a class discussion of the order in which the parts of each group's presentation would be given. This led to the suggestion of producing a written program, the purpose of which was agreed to be that of "preparing [the] audience for what's coming". Then, with the teacher acting as chair and recorder of decisions, the class went on to consider the criteria to be used in evaluating their current drafts. Viewed from the perspective of literacy learning, this reviewing process had the function of encouraging the students to ask themselves questions that required them to adopt a variety of orientations to the texts they had created: were they organized in such a way as to be effective in conveying a sense of the novel studied (functional)? Were they conventionally presented in terms of spelling, punctuation, etc. (performative)? Was the information they contained accurate (informational)?

As the discussion proceeded, various components of the presentations were considered. Finally, they came to the picture collages, discussion of which led the teacher to introduce a criterion which had not yet been explicitly mentioned*:

T: Yes I'm glad you mentioned this because I'd almost forgotten it but I went back Friday night and I was reading some of those things ..
Make sure your text explains your picture ..
Remember twenty-four of us have not read your text ....
If you say, "This is a picture of Sharptop Mountain" .. I don't ski at Sharptop Mountain so what? Maybe my question is, "Are there good ski-runs at Sharptop Mountain?" but that would be — would that be relevant if I asked ... are they good ski hills?

Ps: No

T: You see you haven't helped me as a reader . if you don't give me a little guidance .. and if I'm a skier I think skiing . so tell me a little bit about it.

* In this and the following transcripts, — = interruption or restart; . = 1 second of pause; < > enclose segments where the transcription is uncertain; * = a word that was inaudible; underlining indicates segments that were spoken simultaneously.

> This is important [writes] 'Text and picture — what kind of
> information are you really giving?'
> I think everybody needs to take a look at that to make sure
> you are telling us something significant.

Here, as in the discussion of the written program that it was
agreed each group should prepare, the teacher makes explicit
the need to think of their presentations as communications to
an audience. Their texts do not exist in a void, but in a particular social context: they are intended to be informative for their
peers, who have not read the novels being discussed. Although
this is implicitly understood by the students, it is apparently
not sufficiently well established as one of their text production
strategies for any of them to have suggested this criterion spontaneously in the course of the discussion. By talking about it
explicitly, however, the teacher tries to make it more likely
that they will make use of this criterion as they check their
texts in preparation for the presentations.

By emphasizing the necessity of taking account of the needs
of the audience, the teacher has nudged the class in the direction of adopting an overall epistemic orientation to the texts
they have produced. For what she is asking them to do is to
review their texts from a different perspective — that of a reader
or listener who is not familiar with the novel in question. To
decide whether their texts are effective, therefore, they must
ask themselves not only whether the information is accurate
but also whether it is selected and presented in a way that
makes it interesting and intelligible to the audience for whom
it is intended. Put more abstractly, she is asking them to think
of composing as involving an interaction between two essential goals: that of selecting appropriate content and that of shaping and expressing it appropriately to achieve a particular
rhetorical purpose (Scardamalia and Bereiter, 1985). To approach
the evaluation task in this way will certainly require them to
engage with their texts in the epistemic mode.

In the first part of the session, then, a set of criteria is constructed for the groups to use in evaluating and revising their
material, which requires the students to adopt all four modes
of engagement in reviewing the texts they have prepared.

What is equally important to note, however, is the collaborative manner in which this is done. Throughout the discussion,
the teacher makes it clear that the responsibility for the form

a group's presentation takes rests with the students: "It's your right to prepare your program whatever way you desire as long as it achieves your purpose. 'What is the purpose of your program?' That's what you have to keep in mind." The validity of the students' ideas is also emphasized in the compilation of the set of criteria to be used in reviewing the different types of texts they have produced. However, in introducing and explaining a criterion which the students, on their own, had not suggested, the teacher also contributes to the discussion from her own greater expertise as a writer.

Viewed in terms of the Vygotskian framework introduced above, the whole episode can be seen as an example of teaching as "assisting the learners' performance". The teacher starts by establishing what the students can do alone and then, on that basis, moves the talk into what she judges to be their "zone of proximal development." The complete list of criteria which results is thus a joint production, but one that goes beyond what the students could have produced on their own. As she brings this part of the session to a close, the teacher underlines both the epistemic stance the students need to adopt towards their texts and her conception of learning through collaborative activity:

> You've got your pictures and you've got your idea of who you want to explain it to. Now the next step is just to revise. Add more if you need to add more, take away this if you don't need it. And as a group you can help each other do that 'cause sometimes seven pairs of eyes can see things that one pair can't.

Immediately after this class session, the students went to work in their groups. Within minutes, there was evidence that at least one group was attempting to put into practice the criteria that had been agreed upon, as they asked the teacher to help them resolve a problem that had arisen.

As already mentioned, one of the types of texts that several groups had decided to produce was a collage in which pictures, cut from magazines to illustrate characters and events in the novel, were accompanied by some form of explanatory written text. In fact, it was these explanatory captions that the teacher was referring to, in particular, when she asked the students to make sure they were "saying something significant" in the first passage quoted above. In the group that the teacher has joined, more than one of these collages has been produced and the problem is that, because they were not produced in collaboration, there are both discrepancies and redundancies between them. The teacher suggests, therefore, that they look at each collage in turn to establish how it contributes to the total presentation.

They start with Julie's collage, and the teacher asks her to explain: "Julie tell us what you think you've got here .. what you're aiming for". With some prompting by other members of the group and by the teacher, Julie identifies three categories of picture: people, places, and equipment that figure prominently in the novel. It is in relation to a picture in this latter category that the following episode occurs. In it, the teacher extends the earlier discussion by using one particular way in which a text can be examined to see if it achieves the author's purpose.

T: There's one question I have . What kind of skis are these?
J: I don't know [softly]

[Children lean forward to look more closely. Several suggestions are made, all of them inaudible]

T: For use on what or in what conditions?
G: For — ground
S: * mountains
P: Er — downhill ski
Ps: Yes
T: Are they?
J: No I don't think so
N: Slalom
G: Cross-country?
M: No mountain skis . downhill

[Several speak at once]

T: OK I can see — How many of you people here have ever water-skied?
A: Those are water skis?
D: Those are water skis?
T: Those are water skis
?: * * * *
Ss: Oh yeah
T: If you've never water-skied you might not pick this up
[Several laugh]
But you were right when you said slalom but they're slalom

71

water skis .

er — they have a totally different. er — size and um [Students laugh] and er — binding . but because you have never water-skied you didn't pick that up

I have here somewhere in our books a whole bunch of winter . skiing . er — magazines . where you can get pictures of winter skis

J: I think we saw that *book*

T: *You* probably saw it . I think this is a marvelous idea to have a ski . picture . but let's make sure we get skis for winter conditions

What has happened here is that the teacher has picked up a mismatch between the type of skis illustrated in the picture Julie had selected for her collage and the type of skis that figured in the novel, and she has drawn the group's attention to it as a discrepancy. The text the student has created is not an accurate representation of the text from which she started. From this point of view, it does not "make sense"; revision of a particular kind is needed.

Although in itself this incident may seem to concern no more than an isolated detail, in what follows it becomes clear that the teacher has provided a demonstration of a more generally applicable strategy for evaluating their texts in a way that enables the students to appropriate it and put it to use themselves. For, immediately after this sequence, Danny makes an objection to another picture, pointing out that "it's supposed to be snowing — and it's summer" (referring to the background in the picture), and they discuss various ways of overcoming the problem. "Excellent suggestion," comments the teacher. "Then you get rid of this conflicting information." This is followed by a further instance, also initiated by a student, and finally by the following discussion, in which the task of matching a picture to an aspect of the novel is seen to be, not an absolute matter, but one involving judgment of quite a complex kind.

P: The dog isn't Arthur [i.e., the dog in the picture isn't appropriate]

Ss: Yeah [laugh] * *

J: It's hard to find a dog that's Arthur

G: It doesn't matter * *

?: * *

T: [to P] How do you know how he looks? [i.e., Arthur, the dog]

D: I know * *

72

P: <u>From</u> the book
D: He's a husky
P: Oh yeah.
A: Or Japanese *
J: He looks like a timber wolf or —
T: [laughs] You've got a good point   Sometimes you'll get too precise then you'll — you'll cause yourself to come to a grinding stop because you may not find a picture of a husky with the exact coloring
A: 'Cause like in the play — 'cause in the play <u>it's going to be hard</u>
G: <u>It doesn't</u> say that he's a husky or anything <u>* *</u>
D: <u>Yeah but</u> —
   [Several students speak at once]
G: But in our play it doesn't say the name or anything so . what difference?
T: OK
P: What kind of dog is this?
M: It's a husky or a Japanese ikitsa
T: Or an ikitsa that was right .
   If . if she hasn't found it <u>then</u> —
G: <u>But</u> they haven't seen the book
T: Phuong?
D: <We could show them>
T: Do you think — .
   You've really got a choice . if you can't find a picture of that kind of dog . then are you saying don't use any dog at all or use a dog and say this represents Arthur?
A: <u>* choose a dog that represents Arthur</u>
P: <u>Don't use a</u> . dog
G: Use a dog
T: Is Arthur important to the story?
J, G, A, and M: [in chorus] Yes
D and L: [in chorus] No
J, G, A, and M: [in chorus] Yeah
D: What did he do?
P: He ran away
S: He got . he got — he came back with the people . remember?
G: Yeah . He — he helped them out of the tunnel . <u>*</u>
A and N: <u>Yeah</u>
A: Remember when he was trapped in the tunnel <u>* * *</u>
[Several speak at once]
A: * * out then he <u>followed</u> Arthur all <u>the</u> way round and <dragged> him out

G: Y e a h
N: Yeah
[Several speak at once in agreement]
T: I've got another question . How is it they got lost?
A: Arthur
N: Arthur
T: Is Arthur important?
A, N and G: Yeah
T: OK

This episode starts with Phuong pointing to another pictorial representation, which she considers to be discrepant: the dog in the picture does not look like her personal representation of the dog, Arthur, in the novel. However, as Julie points out, in defense of her choice, "it's hard to find a dog that's Arthur". Some of the other students agree, and the teacher, perhaps conscious that Julie, as the creator of the collage that has provided the material for this collaborative evaluation, has had to accept a considerable amount of implied criticism, introduces an important pragmatic consideration: if one attempts to be too precise, one may find oneself unable to proceed. The question then becomes one of deciding how important it is to include a picture of Arthur in the collage: "Is Arthur important to the story?"

With this question, the talk moves to a new level of sophistication. For, in order to answer it, the students are forced to reinterrogate their mental representations of the whole novel and to compare their judgments of the significance of particular events in order to decide how important a role Arthur plays. With the final, unopposed decision that Arthur is indeed important, the matter of the appropriateness of the pictorial representation is also implicitly resolved and Julie's choice is vindicated.

The episodes we have just examined all occurred in one phase of a larger project, the purpose of which was, in the teacher's words, "to show that you have understood what you have read by explaining the story" through different forms of representation. But "showing what you have understood" is not self-explanatory. What does it mean to have understood a story? And how do you know when you have successfully shown that understanding? By engaging with the students in collaborative talk about the texts that they had read and those that they were creating, the teacher was able to help them extend the criteria

74

for evaluating their success and to involve them in a joint enactment of some of the relevant strategies.

Winter and the Yukon

The second of my examples comes from another extended project, this time in a split Grade Three/Grade Four class in a school serving predominantly Portuguese, Chinese, and Vietnamese minority communities. For two weeks in February, the whole school focused on the theme of winter and, in this classroom, Ann Maher, the teacher, chose to introduce the theme by reading Robert Service's ballad, "The Cremation of Sam McGee". Following the first reading of the poem, the class spent a couple of days in groups creating models of various kinds to advertise a newly illustrated edition of the poem. The group that I observed in detail used an enormous cardboard carton to make a model bookstore with a large window in which many (miniature) books were displayed, together with posters advertising the new book. Another group made a model of the ship's boiler in which Sam McGee was cremated, with a pop-up figure of McGee speaking from amidst the flames.

On the third day, the teacher read the ballad to the class again and then, in a half-hour brainstorming session, invited the children to think of questions arising from the poem to which they would like to find answers. Many questions were suggested concerning the geography of the Yukon, who discovered it, its climate and flora and fauna, and so on. Then, when the teacher had spent a few minutes showing the children how their questions fell into groups corresponding to the disciplines known as history, geography, etc., she asked them each to choose the question they wished to tackle and who they would like to work with, to sign up with their topics on a sheet she had provided, and to start work. She announced that she would talk with each group as soon as they had worked out what they wanted to do.

The task for each group, therefore, was to carry out research on their chosen topic and to find some way of representing what they discovered so that it could be shared with other people; the final outcome of their work would be the presentation of their projects at a parents' open evening two or three weeks later. Written texts were certainly included in the types of outcome the teacher expected, but she encouraged the children to explore other modes of representating, including models, diagrams, and so on. One girl even produced a tape-recorded set of instructions on how to perform a simple experiment she had set up to show how wind is the result of convection currents created by the heat from the sun.*

Long before one begins to think about the final mode of textual presentation, however, the first problem to be solved is that of defining one's topic or, in the case of an inquiry-based project, of identifying the question to be researched. For nine- and ten-year-olds this may be a challenge not encountered before — as it was for Brian and Kim, two nine-year-old Chinese-Canadian students. And when one is still learning the language of the classroom, as they were, the challenge is even more daunting. Aware of their probable difficulty, therefore, the teacher does not wait for them to come to her but calls them for a conference to help them find a topic. "Do you want to come here and think about what projects you're going to work on?" she asks. "What really interests *you*? Things about the animals, the people?"

How do you know which questions you would be interested in researching? What is research, anyway? And where do you find researchable questions? Couched in the language of the classroom, these are questions to which the two boys' previous experience provides no answers. Of course, they have discovered a great deal that has interested them by observing, experimenting, and asking questions about the objects and events that they have incidentally encountered in their homes and community. But it is a very different matter to be asked deliberately to choose a topic to work on in the more formal, text-oriented context of the classroom. Initially, then, the two boys can think of nothing to say in response to the teacher's question.

The teacher, on the other hand, believes on the basis of past experience that most questions become interesting once one has made a commitment to trying to find answers to them. However, she also knows that enthusiasm is more likely to develop if the questions can grow out of an existing interest. Her first problem, therefore, is to find a point of departure. Brian has already written down one or two questions which provide

* A much fuller account of this project and of some of the talk that occurred at crucial points in the work of one or two of the groups is to be found in Chang and Wells (1988).

some possible leads, but he does not seem to be particularly enthusiastic about any of them. For his part, Kim has so far expressed no ideas at all. However, it is as they are considering the possibility of studying the history of the Yukon (the teacher's gloss on one of Brian's questions) that she remembers seeing Brian looking at an atlas. "You're interested in maps too, aren't you, Brian?" she asks, and he nods in agreement. "I wonder if there's some way you could work on the map of the Yukon too — d'you think that would fit into your question?" At that point, Kim asks about Tennessee (the original home of Sam McGee) and the teacher, seeing a possible starting point, suggests that they fetch the globe and try to locate Tennessee and the Yukon.

Some minutes later, after the boys have had a chance to explore the globe, the teacher rejoins them and, together, they look for Yukon and Tennessee and note the distance between them. Looking further afield, the boys notice with surprise how small Britain is and they talk some more about other countries, their size, and the distance between them. Finally, the teacher, who has been answering another child's question, turns back to them and tries to move them towards a decision:

T: OK I want to talk to you two .
   Now you've spent . a lot of time looking at the globe haven't you? ..
   You look both very interested in maps . I wonder . if you could try . and draw a map as part of your project?
   Would that interest you?
   [B and K look dubious]
T: You could do * *
B: Too hard
T: For you? Well how about —
B: Tracing?
T: Tracing? . Pretty small that's the only trouble isn't it?
   [Two inaudible utterances]
T: Would you feel brave enough to try to DRAW one to make it larger?
   You could just use a scrap of paper and try it out . do a rough copy to see how it works
   You never know it might work * * * Want to try a rough copy?
B: [still somewhat reluctant] <I don't know>
T: Well who's going to know if you don't know?

How about you Kim? Do you want to try?

K: * * * *

T: It's a good idea to try it out
If you want to go to the cupboard and just take a piece of .
you know the big paper . the newsprint . just for a rough copy
    OK? and see how it works out . If you don't try it you'll
never know

B: OK

Were they pushed or did they jump? Probably both; for, despite their apparent interest in maps, without the teacher's articulation of the first steps to take and her insistence that they give it a try, they might have remained forever on the brink. However, to pose the issue in terms of an either/or question is to misunderstand the essentially collaborative nature of the teaching-learning relationship, as this was explicated by Vygotsky. Left to their own devices, he points out, learners are limited to the competences that they have already acquired. (In the present instance, for Brian and Kim these do not include being able to choose a topic they would be interested in exploring.) The role of the teacher, therefore, is to engage with the learner in a task that is slightly beyond his current capability and, by "assisting his performance" in that task, to "awaken and rouse to life those functions which are in a state of maturing or in the zone of proximal development" (Vygotsky, 1956). Viewed in this way, the choice of maps as a topic to be explored is a shared achievement and one which, with further such collaborative experiences, Brian and Kim will be able to undertake on their own.

The appropriateness of this analysis of the episode just described is borne out by what follows. Having been helped to get launched into their project, the two boys become fully involved. First, they succeed in drawing a very creditable map of Canada, on which they mark the Yukon and some major cities. Then they each go on to create a boardgame, based on the knowledge they have gained, in which players advance their pieces according to their ability to correctly answer questions about Canadian geography.

Two weeks later, as the groups are completing their projects, the teacher meets with Brian and Kim again to discuss the form their final presentation will take. By this stage, the group includes another Asian boy, Luke, who joined them shortly after the episode described in the previous paragraphs. Having negotiated what remains to be done, the teacher suggests that Kim might like to write about how they came to carry out the project and this leads to the following retrospective review:

T: Kim do you think maybe you could write about . how you boys did this project?
L: How many days we finished in?
T: [dubiously] Yes . and what you did .
Remember back when we started the project?
I remember way back when — when we were writing questions up here [referring to class brainstorming session at the beginning of the thematic unit] . and I think it was you Brian who was interested in maps to start with . is that right?
B: [nods]
T: Right Luke?
L: Yeah.
T: Yeah? Remember we talked — that you — Yes I think it was Kim and Brian . remember the first day or two we were talking about making maps and things . and Luke got interested
B: Oh I remember
T: Do you remember?
B: Yes and Luke asked
T: Luke asked?
B: Yes
T: What did he ask?
B: Asked could he join our group to make maps
T: Oh and he wanted to join the group?
B: Yeah
T: D'you remember that Luke . Right . and you started to make maps?
B: Yeah
T: Remember how you started? What did you do first?
B: Well we started the <dots> . on the —
L: No not that
T: Oooh [expressing great interest]
L: That was the second
T: Was that the second? Following the dots . that was on the —
B: First you told us to try and make one [i.e., a map]
T: Yeah oh I remember . you —
B: And the — and the other day — day . you got the other map for us
T: Oh yes, that big one
B: This one [pointing to the large atlas]
T: [answers a question asked by another student]

79

Right . and you got the big one and then you <u>traced</u> <u>the</u> —
B: <u>And you told us to trace from dots</u>
T: <u>You're right about the dots I remember</u>
So that you know which province was which
L: Then we traced it over then we got this map [i.e., the large one that they are going to display with their games]
T: And then you got the big map uh-huh
L: Yeah
T: And then <u>what did you do?</u>
B: And somebody got the idea of making a game
T: Yeah I don't know where that game — that game idea came from . Do you remember? <u>*</u> <u>*</u> <u>*</u>
B: <u>From a magazine</u> * . I think Annie
T: Pardon dear?
B: I think it's Annie's
T: Oh I remember we were sitting together in a group and we were thinking about how we could finish projects
B: And then the < pattern > Luke want to make a game and I said "No. takes lots of time".
T: [laughs]
B: <u>— and I think</u> it all over that I made it . then we decided to make a map game
T: Yeah yeah . so that's how your project — you changed your ideas and it sort of grew didn't it . <u>with</u> all your ideas?
B: <u>Yeah</u>
T: Interesting ..

In this conversation, the evolution of the finished texts — map and boardgames — is reconstructed so that the boys can see how their ideas originated and developed. By getting them to talk about the processes involved, the teacher brings the boys to the level of conscious awareness so that they can reflect upon what they have been doing. In the light of their initial uncertainty and reluctance to commit themselves, some important points emerge: 1) it is not necessary to have a fully worked-out idea of the end-point in order to get started; 2) new ideas present themselves as one works on one's material, some of which may be worth developing further; 3) revision of one's goals, as well as of the actual text, is a normal and important part of carrying out any project; and 4) a topic often becomes more interesting the more one works on it.

The teacher also talked with the other groups, giving each the assistance that she judged most relevant to the topics they had chosen and their ability to handle them. The final outcomes of their projects varied considerably in quality, of course, as might be expected in a class differing so much in age and previous experience. However, through the activities involved in carrying out their projects, and through the conferences they had with their teacher, all the children encountered important principles about learning through inquiry. And what was most important, those principles were encountered, not in an abstract lecture, but in their enactment in joint activity and in the talk that accompanied it.

Shortly after the parents' evening, at which the children presented their projects and answered questions about what they had been doing, I met with the teacher to review the material I had collected. As we looked at the video recordings I had made of the class at work, and at the transcripts of her meetings with the different groups, she commented,

> It's just like that business that kids need time to talk about what they're going to write about, to work out their ideas, and then to do rough copies to find out what they really think, and then revise. That really interested me. . . that nudging them to make the connection between two ideas, asking them what their topic is — I mean it's the same as the writing process — having them tell you what they're doing, where they're going, what their questions are . . . and having them review the process.

As this teacher had implicitly realized, literacy is a way of using external representations — models, maps, and even games, as well as written texts — as a medium for exploring and developing ideas, for recording what one has come to know, and for representing that information in a form that is interesting to others. This is what she was enabling children to learn about the power of texts as, over the year, she provided experiences in which reading, writing, action, feeling, and thinking were brought to bear on topics that they found interesting and challenging. And, as a result, they became engaged in activities that, at a level appropriate to their ability, involved them, at critical moments, in adopting an epistemic stance to the texts that they were creating. However, of equal significance for the children's development as literate thinkers, Ann Maher was aware of the importance of collaborative talk for students, both with herself as teacher and with each other, about how the various texts they were using and creating could contribute to their achievement of understanding.

81

Teachers as Learners

In the previous two sections, I have presented examples of classrooms in which talk about texts provided opportunities for students to appropriate the inner, invisible mental activities that are at the centre of literacy. Because these activities are not apparent in the surface behavior of a person who is engaging with a text, they are more appropriately made available to learners through talk about activities in which the learner is also engaged as a partner in a collaborative enterprise. This is what is meant by describing learning in school as an intellectual apprenticeship, in which students are drawn into the practices and modes of discourse of the various discipline-based communities of scholars that are valued in the culture and, through assisted performance, enabled to appropriate those practices and modes of discourse and make them their own.

The two teachers from whose classrooms these examples were taken showed in their practice that, implicitly at least, they understood and shared the theory of literacy and learning which I have attempted to present in this paper. However, there are still many whose practice is based on quite different principles. In their classrooms, a rather limited conception of literacy seems to underlie the activities that students undertake, and talk tends to be organized around the *transmission and assessment* of information rather than collaboration in its *transactional construction*. As a result, students often fail to display their full potential, and their shortcomings as learners are attributed to inadequacies in their home and community backgrounds or to their own limited abilities, rather than to the absence of challenging and engaging opportunities to make sense of new ideas and events in the activities that are provided for them in the classroom.

The question, then, is how to persuade these teachers to create, in their classrooms, communities of active inquirers, who exploit the full potential of literacy to empower their learning. Or, in more general terms, how does one bring about educational change in schools? It is to a consideration of this question that I wish to turn in the final section of this paper.

The first point to emphasize is that, if the principles of learning that have been set out above are valid, they apply to teachers as much as they do to children. Indeed, it is doubly important, if teachers are to learn to apply these principles in their curriculum planning and in its enactment, that they experience those same principles in action in their own continuing education. If there is to be a change in classroom practices, therefore, it cannot be brought about in a mechanical way, but must be the result of a change in teachers' ways of thinking about their role in relation to their students' learning. This conclusion is amply demonstrated in the recent research on implementing educational change, which has shown that, where educational innovation is imposed from above without teacher participation at the stages of selecting the changes to be made and planning the means of implementation, the desired changes are at best short-lived and at worst subtly but systematically rejected (Fullan, 1982). The only effective way of bringing about educational change, therefore, is through the professional development of teachers.

Until recently, two basic approaches have been taken to further professional development. In the first, the emphasis has been placed on practice. According to those who advocate this approach, what matters most is that teachers should behave in the "correct" ways, and so, through training courses, practical workshops, and demonstrations, attempts have been made to modify actual teaching behaviors. In the second approach, the emphasis has been placed on theory, on the grounds that only when teachers hold appropriate beliefs will they modify their practice in the desired manner. Both approaches, however, have failed to bring about the desired changes.

The reasons for the ineffectiveness of the first approach have already been suggested. New modes of behavior are not incorporated into existing repertoires unless the patterns to be learned are perceived to be functional, meaningful, and relevant. That is, they must grow out of the teacher's evaluation of the situation as one which is problematic and in need of change. Furthermore, the change proposed must be grounded in theory. To that extent the proponents of the second approach are correct in placing an emphasis on theory. But theory that does not grow out of first-hand experience may all too easily remain inert and so have no effect in bringing about change in practice. What is needed, therefore, is an approach to teachers' further professional development that recognizes, first, that learning is a matter of individual, incremental construc-

83

tion and must therefore be based on each teacher's current understanding and, second, that theory and practice stand in a dialectical relationship to each other, each influencing and being influenced by the other. The implication of these principles is that the most effective professional development will be classroom-based and problem-oriented. In other words, the emphasis will be on enabling teachers to acquire the competences and resources to be systematic and intentional learners in and about their own professional situations, and to acquire the confidence and disposition to use them (Duckworth, 1987; Connelly and Clandinin, 1988).

In the last few years, a variety of new approaches have been adopted that attempt to meet these conditions, under such titles as "classroom inquiry", "teacher as researcher", and "collaborative action research". What all have in common is the recognition of the importance of treating the teacher as an agent of change with respect to her or his own learning, whilst at the same time providing some form of professional support. In the following paragraphs I should like to describe one approach that has grown out of our work on the development of literacy. Indeed, as I shall try to show, this approach is in itself an exemplification of how understanding is empowered through an epistemic engagement with text. To make this connection, however, I shall need to extend somewhat further the definition of "text" that has been developed in the preceding pages.

A written text, it has been argued, functions as a "cognitive amplifier" (Bruner, 1972) in providing an external and fixed representation of the outcome of intentional mental processes, which can be read, reflected upon, revised, and rewritten. In the process, the writer's understanding of the topic may be significantly enhanced, as may be that of readers, if they share the cultural conventions that enable them to construct an interpretation. On the same basis, as has already been argued, orally produced texts, if they are recorded or recalled verbatim, and other forms of symbolic representation, such as models, paintings, and films, can perform a similar function. And so, by a further extension, can audio and video recordings of classroom activities, when they are treated as "texts" which may be interpreted, reflected upon, and made the basis for revised classroom practice.

The recognition of the potential of video recordings to

function in this way as "reflective texts" emerged gradually from a number of classroom inquiries in which researchers collaborated with teachers on topics that arose during our longitudinal study of language and learning in four elementary schools in Toronto. Indeed, each of the teachers from whose classrooms the preceding examples were taken was involved in such an inquiry. Overall, the topics that were addressed varied quite widely. In one school, for example, they ranged from a comparison of different ways of organizing opportunities for children to engage in learning cooperatively, through an exploration of ways of integrating reading and writing with a practical study of energy, to an investigation of the advantages and disadvantages of different ways of giving feedback to children on their writing. Just as the topics varied, so did the teachers' reasons for addressing them. In some cases, the impetus came from outside the classroom — a suggestion or recommendation from a consultant or a workshop leader to try a pedagogical technique new to the teacher concerned. In other cases, the impetus came from the teacher's reflection on her or his own teaching: a specific question was formulated and methods of data collection and analysis were designed to answer the question.

In every case, however, video recordings of the children, as they carried out the various activities that the teachers had arranged, provided one essential component. After both teacher and researcher had viewed the tapes independently, a meeting was held at which selected extracts were reviewed. Under these conditions, with the opportunity they provided for alternative interpretations to be considered and the evidence for them critically examined, the recordings, instead of simply providing a narrative-like account to be viewed relatively uncritically, functioned as both a source of evidence for answering the teacher's original question and as a stimulus to reflection and further inquiry. They became texts of classroom practice, which teachers and researchers talked about collaboratively in order to plan and evaluate revisions in the provision of learning opportunities for students.

Over and over again, in reviewing these texts, what impressed the teachers was the abilities their children demonstrated: their sustained involvement in an activity when it was personally meaningful to them, their willingness to ask questions of each other and to give critical consideration to suggested answers, their concern to produce a finished product that would be successful in communicating with their intended audience. Faced with this evidence, the teachers found themselves having to reconsider some of the assumptions on which they based their pedagogical decisions; and beliefs that had before been tacit became more explicit and, in some cases, were found to need radical change (Chang and Wells, in press).

For many of the teachers, the expectation that they would present the results of their inquiries to a wider audience was a significant factor in the total experience, particularly when this led to the preparation of a written script. Aware of the demands for explicitness and systematicity of exposition that are placed on a writer by the anticipated needs of the audience, they were forced to take the processes that had begun in discussion a stage further, as they tried, through reflection, further reading, writing, and revising, to make their personal connections between theory and practice clearer for themselves so that they could make them clear for their readers and listeners.

In effect, what was happening was that the teachers were engaging in the same sort of epistemic engagement with texts, both written and video-recorded, that I have been advocating for younger learners. And the results were doubly beneficial — as the teachers themselves recognized. First, they were better able to see how, for reading and writing to contribute to learning, the task context in which these activities occur must be meaningful and relevant to the students and one that challenges them to engage with the text epistemically. Secondly, they began to discover how their own involvement in a classroom-based inquiry could function as a demonstration to their students of the behaviors they wanted them to learn.

However, it is their own words that provide the strongest testimony to the value of the experience. I should like to conclude, therefore, with a passage from a report written by Ann Maher (1989) on an inquiry into readers' response that she conducted as a teacher-researcher in a Grade Four/Five classroom two years after the project on the Yukon. Having described in some detail the successive revisions she made to her original practice as a result of what she learned from observing and talking with the children, she concludes by reviewing the total experience:

> What more needs to be said? If we want to learn about what students think, we need only ask, then listen actively. When I launched into this inquiry, my discomfort and dissatisfaction with the quality and quantity of reader response in my reading program led me to examine my theory and practice. Recognizing the restrictive nature of my teacher-centred program, I had no choice but to look for a better way. Slowly I moved to open up my program to allow for the expression of my students' responses to the texts they were engaged in reading.
>
> This inquiry has involved me in the fascinating process of exploring a new way of working with all aspects of language development. My initial statement of inquiry remained somewhat hazy and obscure for some time. Four months later rereading the words, "If I refocus the structure of my reading program from directed group work, to one that is based on the reading of books of student choice, will there be an observable difference in reader response?" I answer, "Most definitely!"
>
> But there is so much more to my learning than that. It is not only reader response that captured my attention, but more central to my interests became the solution to the problem of how to facilitate the exchange and expression of student response. It is clear to me now that what is needed to enliven the reader response in my classroom is lots of time to read, continuing conversations in both oral and written form about reading and writing, and a variety of well chosen books to read. . . . It is the shared experience of reading and writing that enriches us all with the insights and perceptions of the community in which we are working.

Conclusion

In the examples presented and discussed in the preceding pages I have tried to show that literacy is not a single, homogeneous competence but, rather, that it involves being able to engage with texts of different types in modes appropriate to the different purposes people have in using them. In particular, I have emphasized the powerful role that texts can play in intellectual development when they are engaged with epistemically as an external representation of meaning that can be reflected upon, interrogated, and revised. To learn how to engage with texts in ways appropriate to the purposes they can serve, however, children need to see and hear enactments of those inner mental processes that are the essence of literate behavior so that they can appropriate them and deploy them for themselves. And, I have argued, it is through collaborative talk about texts of varying kinds in the context of meaningful joint activities, undertaken with the assistance of a more skilled co-participant, that this learning can most effectively occur. It is in this sense that learning to be literate can be thought of as an intellectual apprenticeship.

If children are to have opportunities to learn in this way, however, there will need to be radical changes in the ways in which most teachers think about the place of texts of various kinds in their classroom programs and about their own role in helping children to engage with them appropriately. For this to happen, teachers need to become learners about literacy and learning through the same sort of processes of inquiry, conducted in their own classrooms, as those that have been advocated for the children they teach. One such mode of professional development, which has been found valuable by those teachers who have engaged in it, involves the use of video-recorded observations made in their classrooms over the course of some curricular unit. By treating such recordings as texts, which can be reflected upon through collaborative talk with colleagues and other educators, teachers have been enabled to learn — in their zones of proximal development — to create classroom communities that provide opportunities to engage in such collaborative talk about texts — communities in which *all* exploit the potential of literacy to empower their thinking and feeling.

Drama Talk

David Booth is a professor of language arts, drama, and children's literature at the Faculty of Education, University of Toronto. A well-known author and speaker, he has traveled widely throughout Canada and the United States, sharing with teachers his strategies for using real stories for children as the heart of the curriculum. Using drama as a response mode, Professor Booth has encouraged the idea of the interactive classroom where children use role play to deepen their understanding of story and their relationships to each other. He is the author of Drama in the Formative Years, *along with many texts for children and reference materials for teachers and parents. As part of the team developing the Peel* TALK *Project, David Booth worked with teachers in promoting speaking and listening as being integral to the learning process, and helped to develop the companion book to this volume, written by teachers from their own classroom research.*

In his article, Booth outlines the two principles of this art form — improvisation (using our own words to create drama), and interpretation (reading aloud the words of others and making them our own). His thesis is that talking in role can open up powerful avenues for learning, as students work together collaboratively to make meaning, both as participants in the dramatic situation and as members of the classroom community.

Our Own Words and the Words of Others

DAVID BOOTH

Improvising Role Talk

Drama Talk

As a drama teacher, I am concerned with developing effective language processes in the classroom without diminishing the inherent worth of the art form called drama, and with creating useful drama strategies that will help us promote language growth in children. These reciprocal processes lead me to begin this paper with a letter I received from a nine-year-old girl who had taken part in a drama demonstration based on the novel by Jane Yolen, *Children of the Wolf.*

> Dear Mr. Booth,
> I really enjoyed talking about the wolf boy. (Even if I pretty well thought it wasn't true.) It was a very interesting subject. Although I am a shy person, I didn't talk much but enjoyed listening to others while having a bunch of thoughts whizzing through my head.
>
> Yours truly,
> Jennifer

During the lesson, the children's teacher had whispered in my ear, as Jennifer was speaking in role, "She has never spoken in class." But as Jennifer's letter indicates, her own awareness of her shyness, her inability to talk in public, did not limit her learning. And when the context was strong enough, as in the drama moment, she could and would speak.

As we engage in talk, we literally tell the stories of our lives as we live them, constructing the realities of our beings in conversation. As individuals, we must assimilate our experiences and build them into our continuing picture of our world. "The greatest learning occurs when drama functions for the same purpose as language — to symbolize, structure, regulate, classify and give meaning to experience. And the medium is the child himself" (Collins, 1983). The responses we get from talk profoundly affect both the world picture that we are creating and our view of ourselves. All talk, be it purposeful or random in nature, helps us look at the human race in all its variety, and is therefore an educative experience.

It is generally accepted in schools today that talk is a vital aspect of the learning curriculum. As teachers, we must examine the nature of "drama talk", speaking and listening both in and out of role, so that we can understand its impact on learning.

LANGUAGE GROWTH THROUGH DRAMA

Language is the heart of the drama process and the means through which the drama is realized (O'Neill, 1982). Drama may be the most appropriate means of providing the types of speaking/listening situations that curriculum guides now demand from teachers. It can facilitate a wide variety of language uses in contexts that require full participation within an affective/cognitive/physical frame, promoting types of talk important to encouraging deep-level thought, such as expatiation, negotiation, clarification, explanation, persuasion, and prediction.

The very nature of drama demands and embodies language. Many curriculum guides suggest that drama is useful in the teaching of oral/expressive language skills. However, this underplays drama's true role in language processing: the child in drama is inside language, using it to make meaning, both private and public, in the "here and now dynamic", with the potential of abstract reflective thought at any given moment. In other words, the child is using language and thought within the context of the drama frame. This is true language experience. "Children have an engaging interest in what they have struggled to express. Producing and receiving language inside one's circle of awareness is the most powerful tool for learning that human beings possess. Classroom drama is one of the most effective ways to stimulate such language" (Wagner, 1985).

Generally, children in school are not given the time to hypothesize and talk themselves into understanding, to "think aloud". Douglas Barnes (1976) calls this groping towards meaning "exploratory talk". It is usually marked by frequent hesitation, rephrasing, false starts, and changes in direction. This type of exploratory talk is one means by which the assimilation and accommodation of new knowledge into the old is carried out. It must thus be part of every language interaction that

91

is to have impact upon children. Talk can help children make sense "out loud" as they come to grips with new ideas and understanding. It is a bridge that helps them explore relationships that arise between what they know and what they are coming to know. When we are dealing with new ideas or coming to new understandings, our talk helps us make sense of both our thoughts and our feelings. If we can put our knowledge into words, then we begin to be able to reflect on that knowledge, to act on it, and to change it. "Our talk gives us some control over the way we perceive and make sense of the world" (Seeley, 1984).

> If it is the case that mastery of language uses depends on familiarity with alternative means of achieving the same ends, then indeed the only way to promote language skills in children would be to foster their more general development, especially their self-awareness, and to extend their interactions with others and with the world. On the other hand, interference with their language in any way would interfere with the development of the children themselves. Where children exhibit reluctance or apprehension about any aspect of language learning or use, one should perhaps look for a failure of education; and inhibition rather than an inability. (Smith, 1977)

In her research, Joan Tough (1977) concluded that three factors are necessary in helping children reach their full language potential: dialogue with an empathetic adult; opportunities for imaginative play; and an enabling environment in which the child can encounter a variety of languaging experiences. Since these are the characteristics of quality drama, teachers can offer children language possibilities that may be limited in regular classroom situations.

In a drama program, the children have opportunities to use language for a variety of purposes: planning, speculating, predicting, listening, organizing, mapping, storytelling, sequencing, narrating, interviewing, questioning, asking for information, persuading, reporting, giving details, tape recording, elaborating, reasoning, criticizing, evaluating.

> We advocate, in short, planned intervention in the child's language development. At the level at present being discussed this will mean that the teacher recognizes the need for the child to include in his experience the following uses of language, and that she will then keep an effective record of his progress in them:

Reporting on present and recalled experiences.
Projecting into the future; anticipating and predicting.
Projecting and comparing possible alternatives.
Perceiving causal and dependent relationships.
Giving explanations of how and why things happen.
Expressing and recognizing tentativeness.
Dealing with problems in the imagination and seeing possible solutions.
Creating experiences through the use of imagination.
Justifying behaviour.
Reflecting on feelings, their own and other people's.
(The Bullock Report, 1975)

THE WOLF BOY

When I am working with teachers on pre-service or in-service courses, I like to structure demonstration classes in drama each week, bringing in the children to teach, giving the teachers opportunities to observe the children inside drama activity and occasions to work alongside the children in role. During one summer session, I invited a Grade Four class identified as having "behavioral problems" to participate in our new program. I chose a new story to work with, Jane Yolen's *Children of the Wolf*. The children sat on the rug in front of me and the teachers in a semi-circle behind them.

I began with a discussion of books and films they had read, seen, or heard about concerning children raised by creatures of the jungle or the forest, and the class recalled Tarzan, Mowgli, and a wolf child remembered from rumor. I then presented the problem to be solved through drama to the class: "We are a group of scientists who have been awarded the contract for developing a program for "humanizing" a twelve-year-old boy, discovered living in a jungle, raised by wolves. In four years, it is our job to create a civilized sixteen-year-old man who will have a chance at a normal life. The first step for our group is to create a set of priorities concerning the training of the wolf boy."

Working in small groups in role as scientists, the children considered the various problems that confronted them concerning changing the feral child's behavior and values. Different groups developed strategies for affecting the wolf boy's language, clothing, food, education, social habits, and emotional needs. The small groups then presented their ideas to the whole class who, along with me in role as director of the project, questioned them and offered suggestions. The children were building a belief in the existence of the wolf boy, and as the members of each group processed the contributions of the class and altered their plans, they were using talk in role as their medium for learning.

I telescoped time by announcing that one year had passed and now each group of doctors would reveal the progress they had made with the wolf boy. The language of the children dramatically changed as the groups presented their findings. They took their roles as scientists very seriously, and used their notes from their clipboards as the basis for their discussion. Their body language, choice of words, sense of audience, and strength in role became much more complex. They seemed to sense themselves as authorities, as their commitment to the drama grew.

When presenting their findings at the end of year three, the first group announced that they felt the boy should be freed to return home. Their proclamation divided the class and we formed new groups representing the two sides of the issue. The emotion was strong, resulting in a third group who were undecided and stood between the other two. The argument continued, and those in the middle found themselves joining whoever was speaking at the moment.

Unfortunately, the school bus arrived and there was no completion to the drama. The teacher had the children write me letters describing their feelings, and these excerpts represent the range of opinions that grew from the work.

I think he should be a boy.

It was confusing to decide if he should be a boy or a wolf. It was hard I think that he should be a wolf.

I like the story about the wolf-boy and I said the wolf-boy should have cooked food and the scientists said the wolf-boy should be in a white room to be studied and see how to eat the raw meat.

Thank you for inviting us to hear the story about the wolf-boy. We had fun with the scientists. I think we should leave him a wolf boy becose he don't see no one to tell him somethink about people.

It was a very interesting morning. I enjoyed myself alot. It was real exciting. I also learned a great deal. It was a great experience for me and I will never forget that day.

And let the wolf boy do his own choice.

The children and I never "met" the wolf boy: there seemed no reason for his presence. The children talked about him and created him in his absence. They cared passionately about his past, and argued with conviction about his future. Their language grew with the situation and with their belief in the wolf child. In role they were scientists who wore the mantle of the expert; they controlled the direction of the drama and the quality of the language; they had ownership of their work.

THE POWER OF ROLE PLAY

When a child improvises, he or she begins to pay attention to the implications in the statements being made and to the relationships among them. Through drama dialogue, the group attempts to make clear these implications, so that the speaker can see what was and what was not communicated. In any kind of "real" talk, the speakers must deal with understanding what has been said. Drama forces the participants to consider the content and context of the statements, and provides a forum that allows clarification, restating, and subsequent comprehension. The child is using "real" language in "as if" settings.

Role lets children leave the narrow confines of their own worlds and gives them entry into new forms of existence. At the same time, they must find a sense of their own relationships to this fictional life, the "me in the role", and the "role in me". When children participate in drama, they are in charge of building the dramatic experience through their actions and words. They become the drama, discovering ideas and directions that will surprise and change them. Because meanings are being made and not given, the children will find responses and language powers that are unexpected, engendered by the collective drive for group meaning. As the drama is revealed, so the learning opportunities develop, "the creative receptivity of a community of listeners, a chance to lay aside . . . egocentricity while encompassed about with a cloud of witnesses" (Rosen, 1986).

In using drama as a teaching strategy, the teacher must create an environment in which talk is normal and desired, and in which student contributions are valued not only by the teacher but by the other students. Because drama provides role situations different from those in regular classroom settings, children

95

can begin to regulate the action and determine the degree of commitment. This will markedly affect the language use of everyone in the classroom, including the teacher. Modes, registers, and qualities of language can be released more effectively through drama than in most other classroom situations. Both the student's confidence and competence in his or her languaging abilities are enriched and increased through the synthesis between language, feeling, and thought (Stabler, 1978).

When children assume roles, they expand their own language power (Wagner, 1978). The beginnings of drama are in play, during which children are accustomed to learning while in role. When the context of drama allows children in role to initiate language interaction and wield authority, they have opportunities to gain understandings from their own frames of reference, free from the language expectations and control of the teacher. The functional elements of language are affected by the social context in which speakers find themselves. Learning opportunities are altered by changes in the relationship between teacher and children. As students interact inside role, they are able to explore social functions of language that do not arise in the language forms of the traditional classroom. The context plays a part in determining what we say, and what we say plays a part in determining the context (Halliday, 1975). As the form of communication changes, so will the form of what is learned (Barnes, 1976).

THE TEACHER'S ROLE

Alternative communication patterns are set up in the dynamics of a drama situation where the right to control talk is determined by the context of the drama rather than by socially ascribed roles, such as that of the teacher as regulator and instructor. As the teacher becomes a member of the ensemble, he or she is able to alter control of the communication systems in the classroom. The children gain new expectations about what language is suitable in a particular context. The teacher then has a powerful technique to help the students reshape their own knowledge. They can begin to take responsibility for their own learning, influencing the events that occur. The teacher and children begin to negotiate their relationships within the drama framework. They begin to spontaneously elaborate on the situation, contributing language and exploring alternate language functions, ". . . allocating pupils an active role in what has been so happily named 'the conversation of mankind'" (Barnes, 1986).

The teacher's task is to work within the drama framework and assist the children in focusing, defining, and structuring events. The teacher thus monitors the drama learning from within. This convention of role-taking in drama opens up the language, thought, and social patterns of the class. The initiative to communicate is in the hands of the children, and they have some decision-making power concerning what language is appropriate to the learning. They select the language that most closely fits the requirements of the situation. The drama framework allows the children to risk expressing their thoughts and feelings within a social dynamic where the drama rather than the teacher does the controlling. The children are active learners in control of the decisions, and safely in role.

The teacher can contribute whatever is necessary to keep the learning productive — directing and focusing it from inside the group, but not dominating it. In role, the teacher can be an "actual listener", not an "evaluator", and thus has a whole new range of communication strategies open to him or her. The teacher can operate through a wide spectrum of roles, as well as using the traditional teacher options of instructor, narrator, and side coach.

Being in role means that the child is able to practise language codes very different from those dictated by society. The drama context sets up language demands that will vary from situation to situation. Both emotional and cognitive commitment, supported by the drama, will provide stimulus for language exploration, freeing the child and allowing him or her to try out a range of language possibilities.

DRAMA AS INTERACTION

Drama provides teachers with opportunities for classroom talk, but more important, it gives contexts for actual, purposeful language. Dorothy Heathcote says:

> One of the most valuable uses of the dramatic mode is the way it can provide context and purpose for talk, because talk arises out of the nature of situations. Each situation has its own frame, which can demand shifts of style in delivery, purpose of the language, whether public (highly selective) or private (exploratory),

97

degree of precision, and selection of specialized vocabulary. All the variety and restrictions arise from the meaningful productive tension, for the situations are human and must be struggled through.
(Seeley, 1984)

Therefore, the teacher must create a classroom situation that encourages free talk within the limits of the learning context. The objective should be to foster a maximum of individual expression and a minimum of thoughtless or self-indulgent behavior. Through interaction, children present their symbolic formulations for testing against those of others. They express their ideas, in search of reflection and refinement. When children are developing their speaking abilities, the responses of their listeners are an important indicator of whether they have successfully communicated their messages.

Drama is about language, just as it is about thinking. Language is a key means that we have for controlling our lives, for making things happen. Through role play, we can try out different language codes that may lie outside our normal language. As well, role play gives us reasons to notice style and the appropriate voice inflections and gestures that extend meaning. The thinking/feeling mode of drama allows children to reflect on language as they use it, and to engage in levels of abstraction that only drama permits.

Drama is a disciplined art form of inquiry and expression. It helps children organize ideas and feelings about what they are experiencing and have already experienced. It engages thought and feeling responses in immediate, living-through situations. The language that grows from these experiences reveals the importance of including drama work in the curriculum. Emotional involvement with the issues and attitudes seems to stimulate the children's thinking.

Drama is a medium for "out-loud" thought. It gives the participants opportunities for having their ideas reflected back to them while the drama continues. In this give and take, dialoguing in role, the children have their own statements and ideas examined by others in a cognitive/affective frame. The need for communicating within the drama acts as an agent for demanding careful listening, analytical responses, and constant clarification of meaning.

Drama should be an activity that evokes thinking and feeling and language as a way of learning. Its design should reflect the best teaching in the affective and cognitive domains. Unlike many teaching methods, drama makes use of imagery and of abstract thinking and problem-solving. How we balance these aspects may be altered to reflect the needs of particular groups of children. While games and exercises embedded in a large curriculum context may be extremely valuable, they do not constitute the complete range of activities available to the teacher. They may also not be the type of drama most important to language and thought development.

MAKING MEANING

The very nature of drama ensures that children engage in fairly sophisticated thinking processes. The first element that trains thinking skills and a controlled use of emotion is, no doubt, the taking on of another person's perspective, or a "role" as it is called. The perspective that the children take is then used in the service of other types of thinking. In order to perform the drama, the children must learn more than specific facts. They must also engage in the thinking skills that process information and translate it into the drama form. They must draw on their imagery and experience and seek to communicate it to others. The perspective-taking experience in an imagined context requires children to translate their learning into responses understandable to others.

The primary aim of drama should be to help children extract new meanings from their experience and to communicate those meanings in the form of efficient, coherent responses. In this sense drama is both a subject matter and a teaching approach of inherent value to the school curriculum.

Drama can provide an evocative context for the expansion of feelings and ideas, and it demands clarity and force of rhetoric in that expression. Children create alternative selves, alternative lives, and alternative worlds — in play, in storytelling, and in drama. In this way they modify and supplement their everyday experiences. Drama encourages children to bring their understanding of the outside world into the classroom as they deal with the problems and decisions that arise in the drama, through the medium of talk. Whether they are scientists or wolf children, drama talk is a means of giving shape to thought, both within and without the drama.

> We are the meaning makers — every one of us: children, parents, and teachers. To try to make sense, to construct stories, and to share them with others in speech and in writing is an essential part of being human. For those of us who are more knowledge-able and more mature — parents and teachers — the responsi-bility is clear: to interact with those in our care in such a way as to foster and enrich their meaning making.
> (Wells, 1986)

Interpeting the Words of Others

If improvised drama encourages children to make discoveries using their own language, reading aloud can help them do so using the language of others. Traditionally, children have read aloud in order to check pronunciation and syntactic compre-hension. Often, the oral reading preceded discussion or the written answering of comprehension questions. However, the skills embedded in oral interpretation are complex, to say the least, and for many children, oral reading has not led to deeper or stronger interpretation of print, but to word-calling and to correcting the pronunciation of others in the group. The repeated reading aloud of a story as a rote exercise may even decrease a child's understanding of the meaning and apprecia-tion of the story and the words. For these and other reasons, reading aloud by children has been abandoned by some dedi-cated teachers in the cause of student-centred teaching; and yet oral interpretation, when done well, can improve all the skills of comprehension, lead to revelation for the reader, and strengthen the grasp of a particular interpretation on the part of the listener.

Without opportunity to interrogate the text, to rub up against it, to notice how others are feeling and wondering, to question private belief, to expand information, and to hear the voices of print struggling for freedom, the child will be sharing print aloud for no real reason. A few children can decode phoneti-cally and comprehend almost nothing. Even these, especially these, need occasion for coming to grips with the meat of the story before attempting to share their knowledge. The teller and the told are each precious in this process of reading aloud.

Sometimes, it is the reader who is also listening, learning through the ear and the eye at the same time.

Can we as teachers give children the strengths required for oral reading, so that they will approach the process with interest and excitement, accepting the challenge of bringing someone else's words to life, and the risk of discovering a means of communicating learning? Perhaps this is the most complicated and sophisticated of all response modes. Teachers need to re-examine their motives and strategies for including or excluding oral reading in the language programs of their classes.

For example, when a poem is read aloud, the heart and core of the poem emerges. The rhythm or beat of the poem relates to and reinforces the message. Whether the poet uses the cadences of natural speech, the formal unit of literary phrases, repetition, alliteration, onomatopoeia, or rhyme and repetition, the children will come to realize that any of these qualities can create the effect of a poem.

Although reading aloud is not necessary for proficient reading comprehension, it can stimulate learning. It shows children how they can manipulate a text, and trains their eyes and ears in exploring the rhythms of language. Reading aloud lets children demonstrate their reading comprehension, and encourages them to try out new language styles and patterns. Oral reading also verifies print, helping silent readers to "hear" dialogue.

Reading drama in particular requires careful attention and hard work. Until the development of drama in education, script was the natural factor relating drama and text. Unfortunately, it is also the most difficult of the reading activities, especially if the script is long or complex. In the philosophy of Dorothy Heathcote, the students have to penetrate someone else's written words and illuminate those words from their own experience. Then, using their memory, observation, and perception, they have to invent complete characterizations, while remaining true to those suggested by the writer. They also have to memorize and deliver the scripts to an audience, sounding as if they were creating the lines spontaneously. The students must be able to read the script; not to be locked into one meaning; to enjoy the script's content and style; and to relate it to their own life experiences. If print has been a normal part of their lives, if exploring meanings in text and responding has been an integral part of learning, the students will have been part of the reading process (Barton, 1978).

Much of the meaning of a play is in the subtext, the meaning that lies beneath the apparently logical order of the words in the text (Lundy, 1983). In life, actions and words usually have an obvious and unambiguous meaning, but underneath there is a whole range of motives and impulses that support or conflict with the obvious surface meaning.

Reading aloud can be connected to drama in four ways: by sharing rehearsed selections that may lead to dramatic exploration; by reading aloud selections that have previously been the basis for dramatic exploration; by reading aloud in-role items within the drama (letters, proclamations, points of debate, songs, and chants); and by reflecting orally about the drama from personal journals, poems, and related materials that may illuminate the work. Oral interpretation is a complex and difficult task entailing close textual analysis and the communication of a felt artistic response. Most children need assistance in working in an oral reading situation, and drama strategies may provide the teacher with support in this area.

Few scripts for children to read aloud are available (the writers of children's literature generally choose other genres). However, novels, poems, and picture books written for children are an excellent source of good dialogue that may easily be adapted for oral reading activities. Children can work in pairs or in small groups, reading the dialogue silently and then aloud. Teachers can have the children change roles; they can introduce new settings or new tensions; they can change the time period and use various other means to help children dramatize the selection in such a way that they can discover new meanings in it.

In choral reading, the children can explore the sounds and rhythms of language as they interpret poems, songs, chants, and excerpts from children's literature. However, many children need an extra incentive to enjoy the experience of choral reading. Dramatization of the selection may provide this, helping children feel the music and meaning of the words as they bring the author's ideas and themes to life.

Here are some suggestions for read-aloud activities with children.

1. They can join in by reading songs, verses, and poems aloud.

2. They can be part of the choral speaking of poems and rhythmic stories, safely hidden from the critical ears of those who might hinder the process.

3. They can read big book stories or favorite lines from selections on overhead transparencies and chart paper.

4. They can read their own writings aloud in small groups only after editing their print to permit ease in reading.

5. They can work with a buddy from an older class, someone who will offer an experienced shoulder to lean on as they read to each other, and delve deeply into the context of the story as they find ways to bring it to life.

6. They can read the dialogue of a story in groups as if it were from a script. The narrator will give them clues as to how to interpret the words. They can share excerpts from story novels with others who have not read them, so that the listeners will be attentive.

7. They can read aloud sentences, phrases, and words that are useful in proving a point during story discussion, responding with the words of others to support their own ideas and viewpoints.

8. They can read aloud in an assessment situation, one-on-one with the teacher or diagnostician, without rehearsal and without the embarrassment of peers listening in. Adding uninvolved listeners to a testing situation will alter the character of the situation and skew the results.

9. They can read aloud findings from their research activities to other interested children. Perhaps different groups have explored various aspects of a theme or topic, and want to hear from each other to expand their knowledge. They can transfer their findings to overhead transparencies or large charts and share the information by reading aloud. They can read aloud inside the drama frame, using words that they have created through role play, rules, statements, findings — or words they have found in excerpts, letters, documents, tales. This role reading gives added strength to the oral interpretation; belief and commitment often transcend any limitation or difficulty with reading print.

103

10. They can read scripts aloud (though, as I have noted, good ones are difficult to find) in small groups, first reading silently, then exploring the concepts, finding the voices. Better to leave concentrated teaching to whole-class activities. The groups can tape-record their scripts to help themselves further their interpretive work.

11. They can dramatize poems and excerpts using the words of others, but, through interpretive improvisation, bring to them movement and belief. These "minimal scripts" offer opportunity for partner, small group, and whole class exploration. Situations can be added, characters can be changed, music can be incorporated. The children may want to commit changes to memory, the ultimate act of oral interpretation.

12. They can chant, sing, shout, and call alternate lines or sections of a story. At the conclusion of a particular theme or unit, they can read interesting or significant findings — poems that touched them, excerpts that made connections, quotations from novels that represent universal truths, personal writings from journals or writing folders that they feel will have special appeal for their class. The ritual of sharing and summarizing is vital to oral reading in many aspects of tribal life. We can incorporate this power into classroom teaching.

13. Readers' theatre is a technique that allows the children to dramatize narration — selections from novels, short stories, picture books, poems — instead of reading aloud scripted material.

   The children can have one person read the narration, others the dialogue speeches, or they can explore who should read which line. For example, a character who speaks dialogue may also read the information in the narration that refers to him or her. Several children can read narration as in a chorus.

14. Story theatre is another technique that allows children to dramatize material other than scripts. As well as interpreting the dialogue and the narration aloud, the participants can also play out all the actions and movements in the story. Simple narratives, such as those found in myth, fable,

legend, and folktale from the oral tradition, are best suited for story theatre.

I have been reading aloud with children for more than thirty years now. I read, they read, we read together, we echo each other, we make dialogue into script, we chant, we sing, we demonstrate, we share moments, we delight in words, we repeat, we whisper, we shout, we read and move our bodies, we read and clap our hands, we read to those who can't or don't, we read what they don't have or can't see, we read to reveal information we have found, we read to make a point, we read together as a ritual of belonging, we read from our memories, without print, we read to hear the sounds of language, we read to give others our own print ideas, we read to change direction and refocus, we read to find the voices deep within the well, we read to raise our own voices in tribute to literacy and language.

We read aloud what we've written, excerpts from other stories that we loved or wondered about, words that touch us or puzzle us, tales from before, stories about today and tomorrow, episodes from people's lives, poems that cry out for sounds in the air, letters from friends, stories about places where we have never wandered, stories about dogs and horses and mothers and grandads and eccentrics and children and school and city and countryside, stories of hope and death and wonder and fantasy. We read short stories and long stories and chapters that build up the tension for days. We read stories from album covers and music sheets, blurbs about writers from the backs of book jackets, titles, reviews, and recommendations. We read aloud, we fill the classroom with the voices of our ancestors, our friends, our novelists, our poets, our records, our documents, our native people, our researchers, our journalists, our ad writers. We story aloud.

Teacher Talk

Judith M. Newman is a professor of language arts at Mount Saint Vincent University in Nova Scotia. She is the author of three books on teaching: The Craft of Children's Writing; Whole Language: Theory in Use; *and* Finding Our Own Way: Teachers Exploring Their Assumptions. *She has collaborated with teachers in order to share their revelations as classroom researchers and as developing writers. In her work, Judith Newman encourages teachers to examine their own teaching, and to reflect on their concerns by engaging in systematic self-critical analysis of their instructional practices. Judith Newman has spoken throughout Canada and the United States, promoting the theory of whole language teaching and demonstrating the need for teachers to become reflective practitioners.*

In her article "Learning to Teach by Uncovering Our Assumptions", she describes her journey with teachers in coming to grips with change in the classroom. Using sessions where group members describe and share personal incidents and stories, she leads teachers through "teacher talk" sessions, helping them reflect on their own teaching by examining critical incidents in their classroom interactions and then writing down and sharing their learnings with trusted colleagues.

Learning to Teach by Uncovering Our Assumptions

JUDITH M. NEWMAN

> One day Lee, a sixth grader, was struggling with some compre-
> hension questions from his reader when he came to me for help.
> It was the kind of question where the students had to read
> between the lines and devise their own answers. I told Lee there
> was information on page 42 which might help him. A few
> minutes later he was back complaining he could not find the
> answer on that page. I sent him away telling him to take a closer
> look. A short time later he turned to Melissa, a student in his
> reading group, and exclaimed, "Melissa, let me see your reader
> to see if the answer is on your page 42!"

Mary MacDonald (1986), a teacher in one of my graduate
classes, wrote this brief, amusing story at my prompting. I had
asked the teachers to keep an eye on what was going on in their
classrooms and to bring to class a couple of short descriptions
of incidents which caught their attention. I saw the stories as
a tool for conducting research on ourselves. These "critical incidents", as we came to refer to them, offered us a way of exploring our assumptions about langue, about learning, and about
teaching.

Although she knew it held an important lesson for her, Mary
had a difficult time at first, deciding precisely what the story
helped her understand. After some discussion she was able to
see how she'd inadvertently reinforced Lee's expectation that
the meaning was indeed in the book by telling him to take a
closer look at the page. Now she was able to consider what she
might have done to help him discover that reading is an
interpretive activity.

Our analysis of this incident, and many others like it, made
us aware of the following:

> Everything we do in the classroom is founded on a set of assump-
> tions about learning and teaching, about knowledge, and about
> what counts as legitimate reading and writing. That is, each of
> us operates on the basis of what Chris Argyris (1976) calls our
> "action theories."
>
> Our beliefs about learning and teaching are largely tacit. We
> operate a good deal of the time from an intuitive sense of what
> is going on without actively reflecting on what our intentions

might be and what our actions could be saying to students.

Our beliefs about learning and teaching can only be uncovered by engaging in systematic self-critical analysis of our current instructional practices.

We began using critical incidents as a way of finding out more about our current beliefs and about the assumptions underlying what we were doing in the classroom. We collected and shared stories which contributed to our understanding about language and learning and about our role as teachers. Sometimes the incidents confirmed what we believed; more often, however, we were forced to reappraise our assumptions. What these critical incidents often revealed was a surprising gap between what we said we believed about learning and teaching (our "espoused" beliefs) and what our actions were conveying.

In the beginning, I didn't seem to have many stories from my own current teaching and I was bothered by that. Then, quite unexpectedly, I was inundated with stories. One night that week, finding myself unable to sleep, I jotted down a number of incidents in a notebook.

It was at that point I realized something useful: the incidents which help us change as teachers aren't big events — they're the small, everyday, ongoing occurrences. I wrote:

I can see our learning opportunities come from comments made in passing, from a statement overheard, from something a student might write in a journal, from something we might read either because it confirms our experiences or because we disagree and have to consider what we believe instead, or because it opens possibilities we haven't thought about before.

I also realized the learning remains hidden unless we have some reason for making it explicit. Writing the stories down was important. It forced us to explain the situation to ourselves. Engaging in this kind of analysis alone wasn't easy. We needed to ask one another questions such as:

Why was an incident memorable?
What made it significant?
What did we learn from it?
How might we have dealt with that situation differently?

Only then could we see the point of the story and talk about the underlying assumptions.

Learning about Learning and Teaching

Let me share an incident so you can see how I began exploring my own assumptions about learning and teaching. I was reading Sondra Perl and Nancy Wilson's last chapter in *Through Teachers' Eyes* (1986). In that chapter they summarize what they learned from their study of writing in a single school in upper New York State. One notion which struck a chord was their concept of "teaching as enabling". They made me think about how difficult it is to find a balance between "imposing judgement and allowing for students' spontaneity, between controlling students' actions and offering free rein."

That described perfectly what I was then experiencing with one of my classes. Early in the fall, I'd received an invitation to write a book about the "politics of language instruction". I had extended the invitation to the teachers and suggested we work on a collaborative effort but, while no one said anything specific about the invitation, the body language was definitely saying, "No way!" I let the invitation stand until, finally, one student was actually brave enough to write me a mail message letting me know she didn't want to be involved. Her message forced me to look at my intentions for those teachers, at what I was trying to accomplish with them, and at this particular "assignment" as they perceived it to be.

A number of them, I was sure, were feeling themselves on a very short rein. However, as I reconsidered my intentions, I realized I didn't want to abandon the book just yet. I felt the teachers were ready to try writing for an unknown public audience in order to experience how publication makes explicit the need for such writing conventions as spelling, grammar, punctuation, and text organization. (This wasn't, by the way, our first writing effort — we had already completed a number of short pieces and had compiled two class collections.) I thought about whether I was imposing my agenda on them, taking away ownership, limiting their choices, or whether I was putting them in a situation which would help them grow. I decided to let the task stand, realizing that time would tell. If the teachers were able to find their way into some writing, I would have facilitated their exploration; if they simply compiled, if they wrote to placate me (and their writing would show that — it would have little vitality), then I'd have imposed my intentions and I'd have to deal with it later on.

Frank Smith (1981) discusses the problem of students' interpretation of teachers' intentions in his article "Demonstrations, Engagement and Sensitivity". He argues that students are learning all the time but that what they could be learning may not be what we think we're teaching. My story is about just such a clash of interpretations. On the one hand, I thought I was extending an open invitation: "Write about a teaching or learning incident that seems important to you and we'll see how the stories come together." The teachers, on the other hand, heard me saying, "Write on this topic." Not only that, I was making them feel extremely vulnerable because none of them had ever written anything for publication before. It took quite a while for the teachers to believe I was really just inviting them to explore; that it didn't matter whether we actually produced a publication, only that we wrote with that intention in mind. This incident helped me consider the kinds of invitations I was extending to my students and how they might not be perceived as I was intending them to be.

Mary Jane Cadegan (1986), an elementary resource teacher, relates an incident with one of her students which helped her see the gap between her intentions and the student's perception of the situation.

> Seven-year-old Jason began writing very long pieces which were remarkable for their strong voice, sophisticated language, and touches of humor. Jason was quite willing to revise for meaning and to insert sentence markers. He was also quite willing to circle words he recognized as misspelled. Unfortunately, this resulted in a page awash in circles because Jason knew the invented spellings he was using were not conventional. When faced with the prospect of making a "good" copy from the lengthy revised and edited version, he was overwhelmed. After laboring through two experiences, he turned to me one day and announced, "I think I'll start to write shorter stories." "Why?" I asked him. "Because I can't stand writing all this stuff again. It's too hard."

As she worked her way through this incident, Mary Jane was able to look at some of her assumptions about making what she called "a good copy". A part of her resource room activity involved having students reread their writing for any unconventional spelling. She would then help them with the conventional form, but in order to draw their attention to the conventional spelling of these words, she felt it was important for them to copy the corrected writing. What Jason helped her see was that, at least for him, her insistence on recopying his stories was leading him to choose to take fewer risks as a writer. She had to ask herself what was more important for his writing development at that point in time. She decided to support his growth as a storyteller rather than force attention to spelling. She did the recopying for several weeks, only drawing Jason back to that aspect of writing when she saw indications of his increased spelling proficiency.

A Learner-Centred Classroom

Since the uncovering of our assumptions often reveals a contradiction or imbalance within us as teachers, this revelation is usually a prompt toward not only new understanding but also change on our parts. A direction in which many teachers are currently changing is a way of teaching alternative to a traditional teacher-centred approach. Uncovering our assumptions through critical incidents can help us understand the nature of this learner-centred alternative and how to practise it.

Trying to be what Douglas Barnes (1976) calls an "interpretive" teacher is not easy. Few of us have any experience with anything other than "transmission" teaching, where much of what the teacher does is based on three assumptions: the meaning of things in the world is immutable and independent of observer and circumstances; reality consists of discrete elements or building blocks which exist independently of one another; and reality as a whole can be known by understanding each of its constituent elements. However, Barnes' notion of teaching as "interpretation" presents a quite different view. From an interpretive perspective, reality is inseparable from the individuals who construct it, the meaning of a situation is determined by the situation itself, and knowledge is an artifact of our continuous encounters with the world. From an interpretive stance the educational focus is on learning and on ways of creating contexts which allow learners to make sense of the world collaboratively.

For example, Susan Settle (1986), a second-grade teacher,

explored a situation which helped her see her interpretive role more clearly. She told the following story:

> One particular child, Carrie, had been reading her story called "Mom's New Vase." It caught my attention immediately because it was one of the best stories she'd written to that point. She had included several new elements in her story creating an interesting opening and plot. However, it wasn't until she made a suggestion to another child that I discovered something else she had done. She had told Shawn that he could change some of the "said" words to make his story more interesting. I saw, then, she had done exactly that herself. Later, I asked Carrie how she had decided to use such a variety of words. She explained that she had referred to the chart posted in the classroom. Chart? It took me a moment to realize she was referring to a chart I had started a week or so before. The children and I had been reading about trade between countries. One child had asked what the word "coaxed" meant. Matt had responded that it was a word used like "said" and we then carried on with our discussion about trade. At the end of the day I had listed "said" and "coaxed" in a chart titled "Words Used in Dialogue" and posted it, thinking I'd use it later when I had an opportunity to "teach" about dialogue. Then I'd promptly forgotten it.

Writing about the incident helped Susan realize that, instead of delivering "lessons" in a formal structured way, responding to her students' queries let her offer information that was directly relevant for what they were doing. What surprised her was the fact that a passing comment and a titled chart could have such an impact on what the students learned. Without further assistance from her, in fact without her even being aware of it, the students engaged in what could be called a "vocabulary lesson". The original lesson had been only incidental. What Susan began to realize was that she didn't have to be teaching from the front of the classroom at all times. She could, instead, lead from behind.

Like Susan Settle, Wayne Serebrin (1986) learned about the resourcefulness of his students and their ability to solve their own problems with just a hint of support from him. He describes a brief encounter with Kristen, a seven-year-old first grader who liked to write about her guinea pigs, Olga and Boris.

> . . . on this day her writing was not coming easily. Kristen wanted to "make a funny story about Olga and Boris" but was having

trouble getting started. She squirmed uneasily in her seat. Shrugging her shoulders, she looked up at me from her heavily-erased page. "Well," I ventured, "how would one of your favorite authors make Olga and Boris seem funny?" For a brief moment she puzzled over the "help" I had offered. Then, with a confident "I know," she stood up and pushed past me on her way to the book corner. She emerged clutching a well-worn copy of one of James Marshall's *George and Martha* stories. I was no longer needed. I returned to the table where I had been writing and watched her.

This incident helped Wayne discover the importance of a timely question. Rather than launching into a dissertation on how to write comedy, his question put Kristen in touch with a favorite author who could show her how to do what she was trying to do. Notice he didn't suggest a particular book or author; instead, in response to her difficulty he merely asked her to think about how one of her favorite authors might create such a situation. The rest he left to Kristen.

These are just some of the powerful insights to interpretive teaching which critical incidents can provide. A number of other incidents yield a more extensive and systematic listing of some of the key characteristics or traits of a learner-centred approach to teaching.

Leading from Behind

This question of what kind of support we should be offering is a crucial one. A comment made by a teacher recently made me think about the issue once again myself. I had just read an article by Allan Neilsen (in press), "Critical Thinking and Reading — Empowering Learners to Think and Act", in which he discusses a problem many teachers have with their changing role. He points out that

> One of the most disturbing interpretations of learner-centered education is the one which sees any action on the part of the teacher as interference with the student's right to be independent and to determine her own destiny. When accepted uncritically, this notion can cause teachers to feel sufficiently guilty or at least sufficiently uncertain about their role that they become paralyzed into inaction. They not only "back off" for fear of being interventionist, in effect they often back right out of the classroom.

Neilsen's comments about the role of the teacher in a learner-centred environment came immediately to mind when Christine described something occurring in her classroom. She explained how her first graders were doing quite a bit of writing — writing in journals, sending mail, and so on — but she was bothered that they weren't actually writing in the writing centre. The children would go to the writing centre, take out the markers, crayons, and paper, and draw like crazy, but they weren't doing much writing there. I suggested she remove the blank paper and substitute lined paper instead. I predicted the invitation extended by lined paper would be different from blank paper. "But I didn't think I was allowed to do that," she said.

Here was precisely the problem Neilsen is addressing: the belief that learner-centred teaching means "hands off". I explained that I believe teachers have an important role in the classroom, most aptly described by Montessori (1948), I think, when she deals with "the prepared environment". She's arguing that teachers have a responsibility for creating a context which offers as many of the desired opportunities as possible; that means building in as many subtle constraints as we can so students are guided by the obvious aspects of the situation.

Take the example of the lined paper. Lined paper, unlike blank paper, says "Write on me!" I'm certain many of the children will create and not draw on lined paper if it's offered. I realize I may be removing some aspect of student choice with my paper selection. If I want to reinstate it, I can create a drawing centre with materials which obviously invite art efforts. Nevertheless, I have a responsibility to set up situations that make invitations as clearly as possible. If an invitation is misinterpreted, then I need to play around with the situation to see in what ways I can influence how the children use it. What keeps this "experimenting" from completely removing the element of choice for the learner is that I haven't said the children can't draw in the writing centre; what I've done is increase the probability they'll write instead. If that doesn't work, I'd experiment with other ways of making the invitation stronger. I might place photocopies of wordless picture books on the table so the children could compose their own text for the stories; I could also offer shape books (small blank notebooks, again with lined paper — perhaps with occasional blank pages for drawing — and a cover of some sort, cut into different shapes:

hearts, squares, Christmas trees, houses, and so on). My point is, it's perfectly legitimate to set up the environment so that specific invitations are being extended.

Sustaining Learning

I've thought about my role as teacher a great deal in the last year. I'm beginning to understand how extending invitations or creating a prepared environment is only a start. We also have to think about how to sustain engagement, how to support students' struggles, how to celebrate their accomplishments, as well as to help them examine their strategies more closely. During a recent workshop with some junior and senior high school teachers I had some useful insights about how I do all of these. The focus of the day was on writing and reading for learning. I'd offered the teachers a difficult text passage to work with, something none of them knew anything about. I'd asked them to read the passage quickly, trying simply to get a feeling for what it was about, and then had them jot gist statements on a small piece of paper. Next, they collaboratively identified what they saw as the elements of the argument. As we went along it became apparent to me, not through anything specific anyone said, that what I was doing as a teacher was quite different from how they perceived their role. They saw themselves concerned primarily with content while I was more interested in initiating and sustaining processes. I was using material with a definite content (in this case about the growth of soot particles in wood stoves), but what I was trying to help these teachers discover was what reading and learning strategies they themselves used and to explore how writing could actually enhance their handling of difficult material. While apparently a rather loose learning structure, what became obvious to me was how much of the situation I was manoeuvring to sustain them at the task and to help them talk about what they were finding out both about content and about their writing and reading strategies. I was helped to see how I was constantly evaluating what they were doing and saying, how I was sustaining their engagement in the activity by asking a focusing question, making a procedural suggestion, or offering a bit of background information to help them out.

Responding to something a teacher wrote in a journal let me clarify further what I think sustaining engagement entails.

Adrice commented on the difficulty she was having trying to be an interpretive teacher. She wrote that she was never sure about how much direction to offer. In my reply I commented:

> What I'm seeing more clearly in my own teaching is that I give a lot of direction, I take responsibility for setting things in motion, for doing enough preparation so that the jump-off invitation will catch as many students as possible. I monitor their reactions, try to follow what's going on so I can help them over hurdles, work to keep them interested, involved, and in touch with their own investigations, and attempt to bring closure by helping them reflect on what they've been finding out, both about content and the tactics they used.

I assume considerable responsibility for initiating experiences and provide a great deal of direction during class. However, the "control" I exert is procedural. I rarely talk about content myself, although I build in loads of opportunities for the teachers to read and discuss material on a range of issues. They become familiar with what major researchers in the field have to say and have considered how these ideas might be implemented in the classroom. I don't tell them what to know or believe; that part of the enterprise is their responsibility.

I try, with everything I do, to leave students enough room to make sense for themselves; yet at the same time, nudge them toward a collaborative interpretation. I don't refrain from "telling" when I'm asked a direct question, or when I think I have something to contribute to a discussion. I also share my musings about class happenings so the teachers can reflect on how I'm teaching them and how they might take on a similar role themselves. As I wrote in one journal:

> Even though I play a prominent role in what's going on, I would argue that we have an "interpretive," "transactional" context going because I'm not expecting you to come up with my meaning — I'm pushing you to sort out your own. I admit I'm attempting to structure the experience so that you may come to value the things I value — the point is, however, I can't ensure you'll end up knowing or believing what I know or believe; that's impossible.

Making Meaning

Gordon Wells (1986) succinctly describes the problem of students constructing meaning. He argues:

Meaning making in conversation should be a collaborative activity. But where there is a considerable disparity between the participants in their mental models and their linguistic resources, the more mature participant has to make adjustments in order to make collaboration possible. Unfortunately, teachers often forget how different from their child's is their own model of the world. . . . Their goal is, rightly, that children should come to see the world from a similarly mature perspective but, in the way that they engage in conversation, they fail to recognize that their perspective cannot be transmitted directly but must be constructed by children for themselves, through a process of building on what they already know and gradually elaborating the framework within which they know it.

This is the perennial problem I face as a teacher. How do I set up a context so there is a gradual movement toward a consensus of interpretation that approximates what I and some of my colleagues currently understand? How do I let teachers "in" on what I believe without giving it the weight of authority? How do I help them explore the contradictions between the beliefs underlying what they do in such a way that they can deal with the discomfort of having to change some of those beliefs? And all of this at the same time as we're trying to make sense of a complex body of research information; trying to make connections between what prominent researchers believe and what we are trying to do as teachers. My problem is the same as other classroom teachers. How do we create a learning context that supports what we want our students to explore in such a way that they are able to create a meaning of their own which comes close to that of the larger interpretive community?

Surrender and Acceptance

Then there's the problem of what to do when everything I try seems to have little impact. Not long ago I was brought face-to-face with the issue of who really controls learning.

I recall the time we were writing "learning stories" and everyone was struggling to get a handle on revising. The others were trying to capture some striking personal incident. But not David. In fact, he'd described an interesting learning experience in a recent journal but saw no connection between what he'd written there and what we were trying to write just now. I mentioned his journal to him when he contended he had no learning stories to tell. Next class he had a piece with him but he'd done little with it beyond what he'd written in his journal. The conference began with him thrusting his paper at me. I slid it back toward him, asking him to describe the point of what he'd written. He recounted the story. I asked him what it was he wanted his readers to understand. He seemed perplexed and didn't answer. I attempted a different tack: how he had tried crafting his piece of writing? Had he worked at making it amusing or serious? He couldn't say. Well, perhaps he might want to think about the point of the story and how he was trying to relate it. "But it's finished," he contended. "Doesn't feel like it," I commented. "But I'm not going to work on it any more," he said.

I had expected that a teacher who enrolled in a graduate course would be prepared to be a participant. I was thrown by David behaving like a reluctant ten- or twelve-year-old, refusing every invitation. There were many times that year when I had to fight the temptation to explode at him. Instead, I tried being supportive, encouraging, and helpful, but in the end he had to decide whether to engage or not. He chose not to. I ask myself if I could have done anything differently. Was there some way I could have drawn him in? I tried a variety of tactics — I shuffled groups to no avail, I tried to help him freewrite, to conference with other students, but his participation was always half-hearted.

I came to appreciate that no matter how much I might want to teach, the students control what they learn. Although I have a responsibility for setting up inviting situations, in the end they determine just what risks they're willing to take. If they reject my invitations I have to dream up new ones, but ultimately the decision to learn is theirs, not mine. I had to accept that David had made his decision.

Teaching as "Research"

Glenda Bissex (1986), in her exploration of teaching as research, attempts to dispel some assumptions about the meaning of "research" and how it relates to classroom teachers. She points out that a teacher-researcher is an observer, a questioner, a learner. Teacher-researchers focus on what is happening at hand; they try to understand the ongoing events of their classrooms: I wonder how much students think about reading outside of class? Teacher-researchers question their educational assumptions; they're continually trying to make sense of their students' interpretation of the tasks and activities they set them: I wonder if children really have to learn to read before

119

they can begin writing? Problems become questions to investigate; new ways of teaching become opportunities for learning: what would happen if I shared my writing with my students? Teacher-researchers are learners; they don't make a separation between those who "know" and those who "do"; they begin to trust their own ability to find out.

What Bissex doesn't mention is the role of "surprise" in uncovering our assumptions. It seems to me the switch into "researcher" occurs at those moments when the unexpected occurs, when things haven't gone as we thought they should, or when our predictions are disconfirmed and we're forced to see a familiar situation with new eyes. It's generally when I'm unsettled about something that's happened, and reflect on it, that I become aware of another critical incident. The trick is to become adept at noticing those moments and doing something about them. June McConaghy (1986), in her discussion of research as a way of knowing, offers one useful technique for capturing a few such incidents. She suggests we keep a running daily log or journal in which to record brief sketches of the stories as well as our thoughts about what these incidents might reveal. Take the following excerpt from one teacher's journal:

> When I sat down and examined what my actions were really doing, I was very upset. I took a long and hard look at what my original goals were and how I could achieve them more effectively. The problem was with the hidden messages which I did not intend to send.
>
> How does a teacher allow students to make their own choices about their learning and still have an accurate view of their literacy development? I find the first step is to have more trust and faith in them. . . . My problem is that most of my controlling is very low-key and at times unconscious on my part.
>
> This is what scares me the most. It is much easier to correct or change things which are obvious and out in the open. If the problem lies in the hidden messages, that takes a great deal more thought. The biggest problem lies in the fact that you must be aware of the problem before you can begin to deal with it.
>
> I have found that reading and writing have helped me go beyond, or should I say, beneath the surface of my beliefs and actions. Sometimes the picture which is exposed is not one I'm comfortable with. . . . In essence, the journals and the readings are acting like a camera — a camera with double capabilities:

it takes photos as well as X-rays helping me see beneath the surface of what I do.

Rebecca has definitely become a teacher-researcher. She's become an observer and a questioner. She has a much clearer picture of what she believes both about literacy and about herself as a learner. She's now examining not only her classroom practices but also the beliefs which underlie those practices.

Changing what we do in the classroom in any meaningful way involves changing attitudes and beliefs, but before we can change our attitudes and beliefs we have to know what they are. The only route I know to uncovering our instructional assumptions is to delve beneath the surface of what we are currently doing. Critical incidents offer us one powerful way of doing just that.

Assessing Talk

Dr. Andrew Wilkinson, who died as this book went to press, was Dean of Language Arts at the University of East Anglia, Norwich, England. He first presented the concept and term of "oracy" in his book Spoken English, *and the successor to that book,* Spoken English Illuminated, *has just been published. He was a creative writer and a winner of the Italia Prize. His university awarded him the degree of Litt. D for a sustained, original, and distinguished contribution to knowledge in his field.*

In this paper, Dr. Wilkinson points out that we have much experience in evaluating students' writing, but not their talk. Yet talk is now recognized as central to their learning, and its evaluation is essential as part of the teaching process.

He examines the oral expression of students under two broad categories: "short turns" and "long turns". The common features of these two kinds of discourse are ideational, interpersonal, and textual. Examples of storytelling (long turns) and group discussions (short turns) are employed to comment on a recursive model of development in both categories of student talk.

Talking Sense: The Assessment of Talk

ANDREW WILKINSON

Teachers have a good deal of experience in the evaluation of writing. After all, students have been asked to write "essays" or "compositions" since the foundation of our school systems. It is, however, only comparatively recently that spoken language has been recognized as a condition of learning in all subjects, and thus the assessment of performance in it a necessity. We have to ask ourselves questions like: What are the differences between the oracy (talking/listening abilities) of, say, average students at Grade K, Grade Eight, and Grade Twelve? Given our current knowledge, questions like this are difficult — but not impossible — to answer.

We may start seeking criteria for assessing oracy by examining some terms in the language we ourselves use. In everyday life we make judgments about people's oral abilities. We say they "talk sense" or "talk nonsense", "have some good ideas", "haven't got an idea in their heads". We say they are "fluent" or "garrulous", are "good listeners" or "just don't listen to a word". We say they "don't know when to stop", "can't organize their thoughts", "don't stick to the point", are "good with words", can "never find the right word". The first group of comments refers to the content of what people say, the second group to their presentation and ability to relate to others, and the third to the choice of words and forms they use. Thus in popular parlance we find some basis for oral assessment.

Most of us would agree that people who are sensible and sensitive talk better than those who are stupid and insensitive; that people who can relate to others talk better than those who can't; and that people who can command and organize words talk better than those who can't. But assessing these qualities is by no means as easy as it might seem. For instance, ability in speech is often equated with loquacity, but oracy is not just a matter of "having words": it also depends on quality of thought, feeling, and relationship. In what follows we shall examine the oracy of students under all these categories. Following Halliday (1970), we shall refer to content as the "ideational" aspect of language, *how* things are said as the "interpersonal" aspect, and the form — grammar and vocabulary — as the "textual" aspect.

Short Turns and Long Turns

The uses of spoken language may seem so bewilderingly various as to make it impossible to classify them for the purposes of assessment. But actually we can make a simple broad division — into "short turns" and "long turns".

In conversation and similar talk — chat, business transactions, discussions — we tend to take a "short turn", and then pause while somebody else makes a similar contribution. On these occasions we don't expect an individual to talk too long at a stretch. In such circumstances the responsibility for the topic(s) and direction of the dialogue is with those contributing.

On the other hand, in storytelling or giving an oral report, an extended account or an explanation, an unscripted speech, or a lecture, it is necessary to take a "long turn". In these circumstances the speaker alone is responsible for the topic and the direction of what is said.

Of course this division is not absolute. Someone may take a long turn in conversation (perhaps to the irritation of others), where short turns are the rule. And a report, perhaps by a child, may be quite short even though it is not part of a conversation. Nevertheless, the general division is very useful, indeed essential, because we cannot fully judge performance in short-turn activities by the criteria we use for long-turn activities. For instance, in lectures (long turns), speakers must have the ability to project and to organize their thoughts over a relatively lengthy period. However, in short turns, voice projection and organization are less important, while listening and responding to specific points are a central concern. (The model by Wilkinson and Berrill, 1990, brings out these differences.)

Even so, there are features which both short-turn and long-turn activities have in common, and it is these which we shall concentrate on. They are those referred to above — ideational, interpersonal, and textual — which we have seen are based on the commonsense judgments of everyday life. We shall see how they feature in students' language, using examples at different grade levels to indicate development. However, it is important to emphasize that development is not linear but recursive. It is not like climbing a ladder from one rung to the next. It is more like waves falling on a beach, one wave making a gain, the next coming short of it, though overall a general advance takes place.

We shall use samples of both long turns — storytelling — and of short turns — group discussions. In examining these samples we shall ask ourselves the question — wherein lies development? There are, of course, many ways to assess it, but for simplicity's sake we shall focus on a few salient ones. Under the category of "ideational", one of the features to be assessed is certainly the quality of the "information" contained in talk; another is the way this information is supported — its "validation". A third is the way it is assessed by the speaker — its "evaluation". Under "interpersonal," the sensitivity of the relation established, maintained, and modified with the listener is important. Under "textual", the choice of words and the organization of the piece are significant.

The Development of Storytelling from Five to Eleven

There are different kinds of story. Here we will consider not the fictional sort but that which is based on the speaker's everyday life. This is, after all, by far the most common form of story — we are always reporting, or reminiscing, or grumbling, or entertaining in stories to family, friends, acquaintances, strangers.

None of the following examples are "set-pieces" — all arose during normal activities in the classroom. The first four are from children sitting informally around the teacher in the home corner, and are part of an enjoyable swap-shop of experiences. The others are spoken to peer groups in which the speakers feel very comfortable. Following each excerpt of talk is a brief assessment of the quality of ideation, interaction, and text. The speakers appear in order of age, and you will note increasing complexity and dexterity in their talk.

Teresa, age five:
I went shopping with my mum. And we went to Tesco's and we went to Debenham's, and my mum bought me a coat in the sales.

Ideational. Information — a general statement, validated by the two illustrations (a supermarket and a department store), serving as a setting for the event.

Interpersonal. Teresa looks at the group unblinking with huge eyes, clasping one hand over a wrist. She speaks quite loudly

126

as though this were an announcement for which she well knows the style of delivery. The second "my mum" is given great pride and emphasis. At the mention of the coat the eyes of two other girls shine.

Textual. A chronological organization.

> Tracey, age six:
> My news is my friend and she's called Jenny. She's in Mrs. Howes'. I don't play with her at dinner time, 'cos I'm a packed lunch, and she's a hot dinner. And that's all.

Ideational. The topic, a friend, is denoted (information), then supported by identification of name and class (validation). The scene sets the main point — the children don't play at dinner time — and a reason to validate it (we're on separate meal schedules) follows.

Interpersonal. Tracey is hugging herself, keeping her eyes down in a solemn face, and talking in rather a confiding tone. This alienation of friend from friend brought about by the system is a serious matter. She receives a nod of emphatic support from Michael, which he continues as though mesmerized. Several others are sympathetic, but William seems not to be. "I like Big Macs," he says, and the teacher asks him if his head is loose.

Textual: Neither children nor teacher find anything strange in "'cos I'm a packed lunch and she's a hot dinner". Why should they? It is their normal usage.

> Paul, age seven:
> We started off, and Gran gave us some nibbles and a drink first, then dinner, then pudding which was cheesecake and cheese, and there was raspberry, peach, and strawberry. Then we all went to bed, and then in the morning we had breakfast. And then we went to a restaurant, and it was *brilliant*.

Ideational. Bare items of information (though "pudding" is detailed). But the "flavors" which seem to support either "cheesecake" or "cheese" in fact do neither. They are a separate item, unstated (yoghurts). Emotion is held close in until the last, but his final sentence evaluates, at least for him, the restaurant and possibly the whole visit.

Interpersonal. Paul delivers in a clear, almost military style,

127

giving the items as a record, until he comes to his final phrase, "and it was *brilliant*." The children like this recital of food; Nigel draws in his breath.

Textual. A chronological "bed-to-bed". (A bed-to-bed is a common form of young children's written composition in which the protagonist gets up, goes through the major events of the day — usually meals — and goes to bed again.) Here the beds are absent but the food is very much present.

> Kelly, age eight:
> We went to Hunstanton in my dad's car, and we saw this seal. It smelt horrid. My mum said, "Come away and let's tell somebody." But two men came in a truck and we did not see what happened. We had ice-cream at the amusements, and I wasted my money. And my sister lost her bag. And that's all really.

Ideational. The first sentence orients us, and then there are three episodes — the seal, the amusements, the loss of the bag. A good deal of affect appears in the language about the seal, and in the tone of voice in the last episode. (Seals were dying in the North Sea from an infection related to distemper in dogs and were being washed up along the coast.) In each episode there is evaluation — concerning the seal in "It smelt horrid" and in the shudder with which this is said. In "the amusements" it lies in "wasted my money" (on the pin machines), and in "my sister lost her bag" in the tone in which this is said (meaning, "She would, wouldn't she?").

Interpersonal. There is a wryness in Kelly's tone when she speaks of "wasting her money" and of her sister. There are signs of dramatic talent, in "smelt horrid": the children shudder with her. And she changes mood quickly for the last two episodes.

Textual. Chronological structure, stopping rather than finishing, in which she includes nothing irrelevant. "Smelt horrid" is effective for the meaning she gives it, and she uses "wasted my money" with a certain irony. The meaning of "my sister lost her bag" is in her paralinguistics and facial expression.

> Struan, age nine:
> Well, when we went to Scotland we went to Benderloch, and we went out to Trulee Bay — you see my granny lives there. And she lives very near the beach, so you see there was this

speedboat on the beach, and this man who owned them let us go out on them. And we took a picnic lunch and it was *fantastic!* We stayed in this little castle, *oh boy*! We went down to see the dungeons, we went up and saw a few swords and armor. Oh it was *fantastic* that was ooh! And then we came back, and we went to another one, and it was terribly — it was exactly the same. But we went to the other side of the island, you see, because it was too far to walk. [laughs] So we had to take the speedboat, and then we came back and then we went home.

Ideational. A general statement about the holiday followed by information about a particular day, explained where necessary ("you see my granny lives there", "because it was too far to walk"). The great strength of this piece is in its affect — the enthusiasm Struan displays for the incident and the way he gets this across.

Interpersonal. Struan is a Scottish boy with a grin which keeps breaking into little laughs as he tells his story. Indeed he is known as a raconteur — phrases like "you see" indicate his intimacy with his listeners. He talks quickly and with enthusiasm to which they respond with large, shining eyes. When he first uses the word "fantastic" he perceives their excitement and uses another "hurrah" term, "Oh boy". They glimmer delightedly in response. He knows he has got them and very successfully uses "fantastic" again. But not content with this he crowns his triumph by verbalizing the tingle running down their spines — "Ooh!" They are eating out of the palm of his hand.

Textual. Struan organizes chronologically. There are two episodes, the second starting, "And then we came back". Here he begins attempts to do the same thing, to enthuse the listeners again ("It was terribly . . . [exciting?]") but wisely abandons it — once is enough, so the second episode finishes tamely with them going home, though he does attempt to put some humor into it. He conveys emotion very effectively in three ways: one is his attack and tone of voice; the second is his use of emotionally toned words ("castle", "dungeons", "swords", "armor" — these carry the message without additional description); and the third is his use of words whose referential content is minimal but whose emotional content is high — "fantastic", "oh boy", "ooh".

Linda, age ten:

It was a few months ago, about half a year I think it was — we went, I think it was in Italy — and we went to a big tower, and it is one of the Seven Wonders of the World, and it was crooked — it went like that [inclines hand]. And there were two hundred steps and we had to go all the way up, and I was the first one up, and I was almost blown off the side when the bells went. You had to put ear plugs in but we didn't have any, because we didn't know we were going to go. Then we had to go down again and then just across the road there was another place, when — I think it was round, with a long round roof on, and somebody came in and it made such an echo. It was very very loud — he was talking softly and when he went in again it made a loud echo. And then after that we went down again, and we went down to the graveyard. I don't know if we were allowed in but we did go in. There were a few graves, and I wish I'd seen some bones but I didn't. I looked in every single grave that hadn't a grave top on, but I didn't find any.

Ideational. We start with the great advantage of unusual information. And further Linda, we might say, answers the questions of the curious (validation): why was the effect of the bells so devastating? Because she had no earplugs. Why was that? Her family hadn't anticipated the trip (evaluation). The affect is present — the excitement of heightened experience : "almost blown off", "it made such an echo", "I wish I'd seen some bones but I didn't". Linda is tentative ("I think it was") and allows for alternative possibilities ("I don't know whether we were allowed in").

Interpersonal. Linda's face, eyes, cheeks are ovals. She talks quickly and breathily and sounds as if it is all "great fun": her voice becomes more secretive when she is in the graveyard. She does not project to or play the listeners as Struan does, but they enjoy what she says because of its rarity and excitement.

Textual. Three separate incidents are connected temporarily and locationally by the organization of the teller and also by her enthusiasm. Each incident is developed sufficiently for its impact to be felt — this is not undifferentiated chronology. Linda knows how to rephrase for emphasis — notice how the last sentence, with its stress on "every single grave", serves to polish the previous one.

130

Jenny, age eleven:

We had a very exciting holiday on Dartmoor this year. This was because we heard in the news and read in the newspapers that a prisoner had escaped from Dartmoor, and he'd attacked a policeman. You see a policeman coming off duty on Dartmoor became suspicious that a van parked at the side of the road, and he went up to the man, the escaped prisoner who was beside the van, and he threw ammonia in his eyes. Now this could have been very dangerous because ammonia is a chemical, and it could have blinded the policeman. But fortunately the policeman managed to get into the nearet town and get help and he went to hospital. And the police set up road blocks. Now road blocks are not blocks of stone in the middle of the road or anything like that, but a policeman will stop you and show you a photograph of a man, the man, and ask you questions, if you've seen the man, or if you've heard anything, and that's all they are really. And on our way onto Dartmoor once we were stopped by a man, a nice young policeman, and he described the escaped prisoner to us, and he was described as being gipsy-looking, small, heavy-featured, and he had a red strip down one of the sides of his jumper, had a shot gun. And the policeman was obviously very upset because he said to us, "If you see him run him down — only don't say I said so." And he must have been very upset because the policeman who was hurt must have been a mate of his and he was very worried. And as we got further onto Dartmoor there were more road blocks, and this time, as well as showing us the photographs, they checked our boot, only they couldn't have found much in our boot [laughs] because all there was was anaraks and picnic basket and deckchairs, and that was all really, so there was no room for a man in there. It all turned out really well, fortunately, because the man wasn't blinded, and although you would think that through all those road blocks there were on Dartmoor the man couldn't have escaped, he did, but he was captured in Birmingham.

Ideational. The information offered is fresh, unusual. It's not the normal prisoner escape as seen on TV but an incident the speaker has been involved in. Even more than Linda's speech, this one satisfies the questions of the curious — wherever an item needs support this is supplied (validation). There is the explanation of ammonia and its danger, the definition of road blocks, positively and negatively (what one is and isn't), the detailed description of the escapee, and the contents of the boot. (Probably much of this is new knowledge which Jenny acquires

131

from the events and which she takes pleasure in passing on.)
Evaluation is taking place throughout, including at the outcome
("It all turned out really well, fortunately"). In affective terms
we see a sense of the humor of the incident as well as its serious side. And empathy is shown for the "nice young policeman", hypothesizing about the reason for his particular distress
and thus the nature of his language.

Interpersonal. Jenny sits telling her story to her friends in the
serenity of pre-adolescence, her eyes merry when she laughs
about the thought of the prisoner hidden with the luggage. She
talks quietly but clearly, sometimes pausing to plan her next
statement: she does not want to leave anything out — and does
not do so. The group participate with enjoyment — "a nice
young policeman" is put in for her girl friends, but the boys
are also enjoying the adventure (what would they have felt?).
But she does not incite them to excitement. They are carried
along by the intrinsic interest of the material, the details she
chooses, and the way she leads to the denouement. Her skill
is that she seems to let the story tell itself.

Textual. As in so many stories, a summary statement begins,
and then it is filled out in what follows in a narrative account
which comes to a climax — the searching of the boot — and
is followed by a denouement away from the immediate incident, in which two possibilities are scouted before one is chosen
(you would think he couldn't escape — but he did). What sus-
tains this extended language and makes it different from the
recall of information in chronological form is the shaping action
of an underlying story pattern.

There is clear development in the stories we have just examined. Those by more mature students tend to have more
interesting and unusual content, and to support it with illustrations and examples. Whereas less mature students may offer
unadorned facts, the more mature evaluate their information
and their own feelings towards it. Again, less developed students may rattle off their utterances, getting the words out being
their chief concern, while the more developed often sense their
audiences and time their phrasing. And the ability of less developed students to construct at length and with unity, and their
ability to make choices of vocabulary, are strictly limited. In

both these areas they contrast with the more developed students.

The Development of Group Discussion from Seven to Eleven

A Discussion at Seven

Young children can converse well before they attend school. Their use of short turns for a variety of social and cognitive processes develops fast. Their ability to "argue", for instance, is a case in point. A dispute over a toy among three-year-olds is by no means always settled through physical means. One child can put a case in favor of having the toy which includes points from the other child's point of view. These children already know the need to validate their statements.

By the age of seven the children's skills have often widened to include the discussion not just of possessions but of propositions. In a study by Jill Shea (1989), a peer group of seven-year-olds was working on a project — building a school for the future. The actual time spent discussing the task was minimal, presumably because the thinking largely went on in their hands as they constructed buildings from pieces of Lego Duplo. The initial negotiation was as follows:

James: I'll do a classroom.
Tom: No, we all do a wall to start off with.
James: We have to make the classroom first.
Tom: No we don't, we make the walls first, then we make the classrooms. We put them in and. . .
Tessie: But how are we going to get our hands in?
Tom: We'll put the top on last.

This is a jockeying for position in which Tom makes a successful bid for the leadership. Even so he is obliged to provide a rationale for his strategy by explaining in effect that the other processes will be possible because the roof goes on last.

As the work continues over fifty minutes, discussion of the task intermittently occurs amongst social and other talk. Particularly noticeable is this passage which starts on the level of self-aggrandizement and moves into more abstract matters:

Edmund: I know that, Eve. I know everything, Eve.
Tessie: No you don't.

133

Tom: No you don't. Nobody knows everything 'cos in the year 2000 —

Tessie: God knows everything.

[General laughter]

James: No he don't.

Tessie: He does because he's got his plans for everything.

Tom: No he doesn't, 'cos he doesn't know that there's going to be a bomb and there's going to be people fall off.

James: Oh, a walk at the edge of the world and fall off. . .

Tom: Yeah, but he doesn't know that there's going to be people fall off the edge of the world. Even God doesn't really know.

Tessie: He does because he's the one who plans to do it.

Tom: God isn't real because I pray to him sometimes and I say please God if you're real make me . . . one of my stickers fell off my wall.

Edmund: It never happens.

James: I know, because he's not there, he's long way up. You can't whisper to him when he's about 5,000 miles up.

Tessie: You can't really say that 'cos that's not a real prayer, is it? If you say something like Dear God thank you for everything — that's a prayer, that's a prayer.

James: Yeah, he can't listen to us.

[Indecipherable noise]

Edmund: How are you doing up there? He doesn't make any gangs or anything like that. How are you doing up there Fred? How are you doing?

Tom: Fred?

Tessie: Well just because he doesn't make any sound, you don't think . . . someday the world just clashed two pieces together, and —

James: God isn't up there you know. He's down there. He's buried.

Tom: That's an argument, and we're not breaking out an argument about God now.

Ideational. These children have information. Their knowledge of the world is developing. There is a reference to the possibility of nuclear destruction, and to theories of the origin of the world. Prayer, Tessie thinks, has its own rituals. On the other hand, knowledge is uncertain — there are references by two of the children to the possibility of falling off the edge of the world.

This information is not inert — it is used for the validation of the points of view expressed. Tessie starts from the point that "God knows everything". She is thus in a position to answer James by arguing that you cannot say he doesn't exist because he is silent: and that it is illogical to imagine that the world was created not by him, but by two stars colliding. "Well just because he doesn't make any sound you don't think . . . someday the world just clashed two pieces together." She answers Tom's scepticism about prayer by saying he wasn't using the proper forms: "You can't really say that 'cos that's not really prayer is it? If you say something like Dear God thank you for everything — that's a prayer. . ."

Tom's position denies a prescient god, Tessie asserts one, and they are trapped in the free-will/predestination argument which has perplexed theologians for centuries. Tom abandons it and turns to the lack of empirical demonstration of God's existence. Edmund's attack is satirical, calling to "Fred", who can't possibly hear messages. James thinks God is "5,000 miles up" and thus cannot hear whispered prayers. But a few lines later he represents him as buried. This may be an inconsistency, or a reference to Christ, though there are reasons for doubting this. In either case the deity is located in space.

Tom's final comment is an evaluation of the way the conversation is going: "That's an argument, and we're not breaking out an argument about God now." Tom shows an ability to stand back from the discussion and comment that it is not relevant to the task at hand.

Interpersonal. The interpersonal aspects of the discussion centre on claims about the omniscience of God. Tessie has the leading cognitive role in that she asserts and maintains her position and rebuts all the criticisms. Tom takes the lead against her; James and Edmund support him, but they each have their own points; also, they are not just combatting Tessie, but responding to one another. We saw earlier that Tom claimed the leading procedural role; he is aware of the rule of relevance and closes the discussion by tactical means.

Textual. The text is coherent because all contributors focus on Tessie's position, and because it is not extended (Tom cuts it off). Even though in places the grammar does not quite make sense ("someday the world just clashed two pieces together"), the language is vivid and clear in the crucial words. The high point dramatically is Edmund's humorously irreverent address to "Fred".

Much of the dialogue of this group has been unrelated to the task set. Yet the discussion about God is the best part of their "school-building" session. Children together for long periods — a year, several years — have agendas of importance to them which a classroom discussion, ostensibly about something else, may provide a forum for. They have personal lives of which class is just one aspect. While their talk may not be relevant to the task at hand, it *is* relevant to the lives and purposes of the speakers themselves.

A Discussion at Eleven

The differences between the discussions of seven- and eleven-year-olds cannot be described in simple linear terms. So much depends on the circumstances in which each group is talking, their interrelationships, their knowledge of the topic, the task, and their interests and motivation. We shall examine part of a discussion between a group of eleven-year-olds on the theme, "Should parents control the lives of their teenage children?" After noting its features, we shall then consider its relationship to the discussion of the seven-year-olds in the previous section. You will notice differences in slang between this group and all the preceding speakers in this paper: that is because this group is Canadian, members of Ron Lecking's class in Peterborough, Ontario.

Sean starts things off, giving a role to both parties under discussion:

> I think parents should have some control over their teenage children. Like they should have some control over what kind of clothes you wear. . . Teenagers should have a bit of control if they want to wear — Joe uses, you know, not expensive shirts. . . .

But then, thinking as he talks, he develops this point — teenage choice should not run to extremes:

> But I think you can't go really punk. I think your parents should have some control if you're really punky — you know, spiked, coloured hair, purple hair like, um, chains, jeans, jackets every day, leather stuff, make-up, you got stuff, you know, ugly shoes, pants with holes in them all over.

The basis of this authority of parents, in his view, is their experience:

136

Because they've been a teenager, and they probably know what's going on, and what they've done when they were teenagers. Parents know best.

This view is immediately supported by Peter ("Yes, because they've lived a life before") and by Jody ("because they might have been in the same situation when they were young"). Trevor agrees also, but goes on to speak of the parents' feelings and desires:

They just want you to get a supportive job and go through school so he or she can support a family with nice clothes, houses, food, etc. And also wants you to hang around with the right people so you won't pick up bad habits like smoking, or drinking, or drugs. Like say, like Bart said here, like people go around wearing leather jackets and people don't pay attention to them because —

Peter supports this point of Trevor's — the shunning of undesireable companions: "Yeah, because they'll stay away from him — there's something wrong with him." But Sean picks up Trevor's first and main point — the effect on the parents of their children's behavior.

Like, you I think should have some say because if your kid goes around vandalizing places and killing, like stealing, well that's going to give you a bad name, like the parents a bad name. Everybody's going to think that the parent did not raise him right or the parent's a dummy.

Trevor is not really listening to Sean. He is following up his own last point about "bad habits" and he interrupts with:

My dad said if I was taking drugs or something, like, he'd say, "I'd rather you drank a whole bottle of booze in one shot than take drugs because drugs are more harmful."

Peter doesn't really want to accept this "lesser of two evils" argument: "Well, booze is bad." In response, Trevor merely repeats his statement, and it is left to Peter to draw out the moral about the wages of sin:

Yeah, like you'll just get sick and puke and you'll hate it and you won't do it again.

This phase of the discussion is summed up by Jody in traditional phraseology:

137

I think they should have control over your life because they brought you into this world, and they're your guardian until you move on or something.

This part of the discussion has been concerned with the maintenance of consensus. But the holding up for inspection of ideas enables Sean to begin to express reservations about the consensus. In reply to Jody he asks what arises if parents' control becomes unacceptable:

I don't think so. That's like, that's why some kids run away, because they don't like the way their parents treat them.

He gets support from Peter, but Jody objects that they are "talking about a normal parent", and when the others jeer at this he repeats his formulation:

Your parents brought you into the world and they'd probably be more than happy to bring you out of it.

Trevor warns that parents can deteriorate:

And like some of your parents they ask you to do everything. Hey kid, can you go to the store and get me a bag of milk and some cigs? Then they give them ten bucks to spend at the store for himself. That's all right but . . . but if they keep asking you like maybe everyday or something to do it going to be a habit. Like people won't like him because he's too lazy.

Peter, who has murmured an objection to Trevor's "That's all right. . .", now comes in with:

Even one cigarette is like, even one cigarette can ruin your life.

From this, and the way the group takes up the point, it is clear that they have a shared understanding, not explicit in the text, that the reward money will be spent on cigarettes. This sets the group off on a tangent about the addictiveness of tobacco and the morality of the farmers who grow it. Trevor is making a contribution to this when he suddenly realizes it's not on the official agenda.

Yeah, that's because people from Canada come into the United States and buy . . . What are we supposed to be talking about?

Sean, who has remained silent during the digression, speaks in a tone of exaggerated restraint:

138

Let me say something, okay? We're sure taking one point and making that point to another point, and making that point to another point, and talk about that point.

Jenny, the only girl in the group, has for some time said nothing. It's as though she is waiting until all the preliminaries are out of the way so that serious discussion can begin. She now comes in, referring for the first time to the extract they were given to prompt the discussion:

Okay, in the play I think the parents should let the teenager take the job because I mean the parent would want the teenager to become independent, and know what a job is like. And —

She attempts to introduce the topic of independence in the context of the play, but the boys do not follow it up, instead discussing anecdotally the age (fourteen to sixteen) at which it is possible to be employed. After some twenty exchanges, Peter says, "You can be six to get a job, you get a paper route it's still a job." Jenny comes back slightly impatiently: "Yes, but that's not the point."

Sean now supports her, referring once again to the situation in the extract:

Yes, it's not the point. As it refers in this play, this kid has got a job. Now I think he should have asked his parents before doing that.

Now the way is open for a serious discussion of the issues. Trevor introduces the matter of bad companions, and the following exchange occurs:

Trevor: Right, in this play the parent doesn't think the teenager should get this job because he doesn't like who he'd be working with.
Jenny: Not who he'd be working with — the people in the —
Peter: The people who he'd be hanging around with. They could be drinking and smoking.
Jody: The parent has warned the teenager in this play that if, like, he got this job he or she would be hanging around.
Jenny: Yes, but the job he or she is taking has something to do with the class she or he is taking.

Trevor recapitulates his point. Jenny insists he be accurate — it's not the workmates but the hangers-on who are the danger, but she reminds the group that the job has a relation-

139

ship to a course the teenager is taking (presumably meaning that there will be motivation not to waste time). The discussion moves on to a consideration of short-term and long-term objectives:

> Jody: Now with all this practising that means it's probably going to ruin this kid's life, and after every work job at night he's going to be practising for his examination. When he could if he didn't have this job and went to school [i.e., college] maybe get a better job after he went to school [college].
> Trevor: If he got that job then I think his parents are right, because if he got that job he might not want to have it any more, and then he can't get a better job or something. He needs a good education.
> Peter: But he's already got a good education.
> Trevor: Yeah, but he'll have to go back to school to get his diploma.
> Peter: But he'll already have it.
> Trevor: No, because it says you have to pass the examination.

And so Trevor validates his remark by reference back to the text that prompted the discussion.

A Comparison of the Two Discussions

Let us look at the two discussions in the terms which we employed to assess storytelling — ideational, interpersonal, and textual.

Ideational. Among the seven-year-olds there is principally a concern with "describing" (offering facts and assertions) and interpreting. In the discussion about God, for example, they make assertions and support them with arguments. There is, however, speculation in the boys' proposals about God and in Tessie's rejection of them. With the eleven-year-olds the earlier portions of the discussion are "descriptive" (again offering facts and assertions), but the discussion moves to speculation arising from the extract.

The question is not whether mental processes such as description, interpretation, and speculation are occurring, but the level at which they occur. And this is where we need to consider the quality of information, validation, and evaluation in the two discussions.

The information the seven-year-olds reveal in their discussion about God is remarkable: there are references to the possibility of nuclear destruction and to theories of creation. They use this information to validate their arguments. What is interesting about their information and validation is that on the whole it consists of things they have been told, whereas that of the eleven-year-olds comes from things they have observed or experienced. They have learned to use evidence, as provided by the text they were initially given. On the whole the younger children do not evaluate their own offerings, but the older ones revise several times in the course of a sentence ("if your kid goes around vandalizing places and killing, like stealing. . ." i.e., "I mean stealing, not killing"). The evaluation by the younger children of one another's offerings tends to be completely supportive or completely contradictory. ("I know everything." "No, you don't.") The older children often tend to accept one another's utterances but modify them ("He needs a good education" "But he's already got a good education"). Both groups, or at least individuals in them, show an ability to evaluate the group performance. In the younger group, it is Tom who brings the talk back to the agenda ("That's an argument, and we're not breaking out an argument about God now"). In the older group, Jenny is the person who is monitoring the others as well as participating, and she does this over long stretches of talk. She merely listens in the first two phases, but initiates the third and keeps it on track when it seems to wander again ("Yes, but that's not the point"). Perhaps her detachment comes because she is the only girl in the group.

Interpersonal. In the younger group, Tom immediately assumes the leadership and maintains it, in both the building of the school and the organizing of the discussion. But equally dominant as far as the argument is concerned is Tessie, who takes on all the boys repeatedly, and is only brought to a halt by Tom's use of the rules of procedure. No child plays a passive role — all are cooperative in the sense of contributing ideas to the discussion. Edmund's unique contribution is a comedy act.

With the older group, there is no conflict in personal terms, nothing parallel to Tessie's combat with the boys. It is the ideas that are important, and there is no single dominant person, though some contribute more ideas than others. Jenny's contribution is accepted and made use of on its own merits and

141

not because of her sex (the use of "he or she" to refer back to the "he" in the extract is interesting.) Participants move in and out of leading roles. Jenny's contribution is particularly useful — she spends much time listening, and on the whole does not say much, but no one does more to influence the course of the discussion.

Both groups are aware of the main rules of discussion. The older group listens more to what each person has to say instead of filling silences immediately, as does the younger group, but even with this group there is appropriate turn-taking. The older group is far more concerned with producing a consensus, and in the first phases members agree with one another to an excessive degree. The younger group is less concerned with consensus and more with leadership. Even so, the rules are observed in seeking it. It is only when Tom uses a procedural device to end part of the discussion unattractive to him, that we see the rules being used for other than the pursuit of the ideas the speakers want to express.

In group discussion presentation is far less apparent than in storytelling or exposition to a group of listeners. Participants often, but by no means always, look at the current speaker. Speakers often look at the group generally, but not at individuals, when they talk. Sometimes they talk meditatively with their eyes down — and the older group did this a good deal. It seemed to the observer to be a way of objectifying the issues.

Textual. The structure of the first conversation of the younger children is not related to the task they have been set. Nevertheless it has a coherence about it since it focuses on the arguments for and against the existence of God. It is questionable how long this could have carried on had it not been terminated. The older group had, as was to be expected, an ability to sustain discussion over longer stretches, a sense of where the discussion was going, and how it could be extended. They were able to work to a brief, even though they at times digressed from it.

The vocabulary and idioms of the two groups differ greatly. The statements of the younger children are unambiguous and assertive ("God knows everything"). Those of the older are marked by tentativeness: for instance, by "I think" (i.e., take it for what it's worth); by "you know" (an appeal for support);

142

by "like" (usually introducing an example or redefinition to support a statement which might otherwise seem too unqualified). Again, as far as stylistic flourishes are concerned, there is no parallel to Edmund's aside to the Deity in the younger group. But Sean provides a real vivid description of a "real punk":

> If you're really punky, you know, like spiked colored hair, purple hair, like, um, chains, jackets every day, leather stuff, make-up, you got stuff, you know, ugly shoes and you got, you know, pants with holes in them all over.

But it is important to realize that this passage is not there for its stylistic features but as a validation of Sean's point about the kind of clothing which would be properly unacceptable to parents.

A Question of Development

We can point to "developmental" features in the older group as distinct from the younger. Members of the younger group confront one another, the older group seeks consensus; the younger children are absolute in their opinions, the older are more tentative; the younger use knowledge they have been told, the older validate much more using their own experience of the real world, and are better at introducing evidence to support their ideas. Members of the older group are more likely to listen to others, and to restrain comment until an appropriate time; they can follow longer stretches of discussion, they are more aware of its progress, and their sense of relevance to the brief is greater. In the younger group, the girl and the boys are at odds; in the older group, both sexes are listened to. Of course, some of the differences between the two groups are due to differences of task and context, and perhaps to the fact that the younger are British, the older Canadian. Even so, there is a good deal that we can reasonably consider the result of different developmental levels. There is a large age gap — four years — between the two groups, so we would expect this.

Also, we saw earlier in the paper that we can discern development in the storytelling abilities of students. In other words, in both short-turn and long-turn activities it is possible to evaluate development.

It should be emphasized, however, that a recursive and not a linear model of development is appropriate. No one ascends to heaven by means of a series of short rapid jerks. Many and varied classroom activities are necessary to give oracy the air and space to grow. Development obviously takes place, but it does not take place obviously. And as our students learn more about talk, we should learn more about listening.

Researching Talk

Dr. Sar Khan is associate professor in the Graduate Department of Measurement, Evaluation and Computer Applications at the Ontario Institute for Studies in Education. He has been involved in research and field development activities in Canada and internationally and has contributed many articles to books and periodicals on a variety of topics related to evaluation.

Judith Fine is research officer with the Peel Board of Education. She frequently makes presentations in such areas as: integration of standardized test results in an overall student achievement profile, classroom observation, use of standardized tests with special populations, and identification of students with superior academic ability. She is author of the Peel Board of Education publication, Looking at Measurement: More Than Just Marks.

This article summarizes questionnaire data gathered from Grade One to Six students during the first year of the Peel Board TALK *Project. The questionnaires were designed to elicit information about the topics students most frequently discuss, with whom, attitudes toward talkative and quiet classmates, and feelings about talk in their classrooms. It is through ongoing studies such as this that we will discover more about talk.*

Investigating Children's Talk

SAR KHAN / JUDITH FINE

Talk plays an important role in a child's life, both inside and outside school. This is a medium the child uses to communicate with others, express emotions and feelings, and articulate views and opinions. Children's talk also reflects the quality of spoken language available to them, and one of the important objectives of education should be the improvement of children's spoken language. As well, the quality of talk provides a basis on which others can make judgments about the nature of the social and academic environments in which the children function.

This paper is based on the results of interview and questionnaire data obtained from students in Grades One through Six. These instruments were designed to determine how elementary children feel about talking to different people in various situations. This study of children's talk was part of a larger project entitled "Talk: A Medium of Learning and Change", funded by the Ontario Ministry of Education.

Structured interviews were conducted with forty-four randomly selected children in Grades One to Three in four schools in the Peel Board of Education. Questionnaires were administered to 603 Grade Four, Five, and Six students in the same schools. As well, teachers in these schools were surveyed to determine their views on the role of children's talk in the teaching-learning process, and their concerns about encouraging talk in their classrooms and about the way students talk.

Results

Grades One to Three
The interviews with primary children averaged approximately sixteen minutes, with no striking differences in interview time across the three grades. Most of the interviews were conducted in children's classrooms over a four-week period in May-June 1989. The sample breakdown was: 34 percent (n = 15) from Grade One, 34 percent (n = 15) from Grade Two, and 32 percent (n = 14) from Grade Three.

A large majority of the students (89 percent) indicated that

English was spoken in their homes. Slightly more than half of these students (57 percent) reported that a language other than English was also spoken at home. The languages most often mentioned were those of Eastern Europe (24 percent), Southeast Asia (16 percent), the Far East (12 percent), and French (12 percent). About half of the students (54 percent) indicated that they themselves spoke a language other than English.

The children were asked to name the person(s) to whom they would likely talk about "something good" or "something bad". For both types of situations, the top three choices were mother, father, and friends; however, these students were most likely to talk to their friends about "something good" and to their mothers about "something bad".

The children were then asked to whom they would most likely talk about a number of specific topics, such as school, special events like Christmas or birthdays, and things they want. They told the interviewers that they would most likely talk to their friends about special events, school, feeling happy or angry, and sports or games. They would talk to their mothers about feeling sad and things they wanted, and to their fathers about sports and games, as well as things they wanted.

Children were asked how often they got a chance to talk in class — that is, giving their ideas, answering questions, and talking in a group. Almost half of the students said that they had opportunities to talk in class "most of the time". The remaining half of the group indicated that they had "sometimes" or "rarely" had an opportunity to talk in class.

Almost all students who were interviewed indicated that they had classmates who talked "a lot" — that is, those who answered questions all the time, frequently expressed their ideas, or talked the most in their groups. The students were then asked what they liked most and least about classmates who talked a lot in class. On the positive side, they mentioned that these talkative children were helpful and friendly, had good ideas, and provided a lot of information. On the negative side, they commented that the talkative students ignored the social rules of talk and were often disruptive.

The students also agreed that there were students in their class who talked "only a little". The things they liked most about these children were that they were quiet and observed the social rules of talk. However, they did not like the fact that these classmates did not participate in class discussions.

In deciding about being friends with a classmate, students said it did not matter whether he or she talked "a lot" or "only a little". Respondents expressed the feeling that they would like to have either of these two types of children as friends.

Students were asked to indicate how comfortable they would feel when talking to the whole class, to a small group, or to only one other child. The majority of the students did not feel comfortable about talking to the whole class — only 40 percent said they felt good about it. However, they thought they would be comfortable in talking to a small group (52 percent) and in talking to only one other child (70 percent).

The students were given an opportunity to explain what things bothered them when they did not feel good about talking to the whole class, a small group, or only one other child. When talking to the whole class, the concerns most often mentioned were: feeling embarrassed, nervous, or afraid; how the other students would react; and not presenting information accurately.

Grades Four to Six

A total of 603 (half males, half females) students in the four project schools were administered a paper-and-pencil questionnaire. Because two of the schools contained Grades K to Five, and two contained Grades K to Six, the grade distribution of the students was somewhat uneven: 37 percent of the students were in Grade Four, 46 percent in Grade Five, and 17 percent in Grade Six.

Almost two-thirds of the students indicated that English was spoken at home. Three-quarters of them mentioned that they spoke a language in addition to English; half of these students reported that French was the other language.

The students reported that they were more likely to share "good" or "bad" news with their mother, father, or friends than with their teachers or siblings. Regardless of the nature of the event, females were more likely than males to talk to their mothers, their sisters, or their friends.

Students were asked to indicate what types of things they would talk about, and to whom. They reported that they would most often talk to their mothers about feeling sick, about things they would like to have, and about their feelings (happy or sad).

148

A significant number of students indicated that they would be especially likely to talk to their friends about TV shows, music, videos, sports, and teachers. These students mentioned that they would be less likely to talk to their fathers about various matters than to their mothers or friends.

Students were asked to indicate how often they got a chance to talk in class. Only 8 percent reported that they "hardly ever" got a chance to talk in class. When asked to mention the things they liked most about students who talked "a lot" in class, they noted that these students offered good ideas, provided a lot of information, and were helpful and friendly. However, the things they liked least about their talkative classmates were that these students did not follow the social rules of talk, tended to disrupt the class, and often dominated class discussions.

Students also had an opportunity to express their likes and dislikes about students who talked "only a little" in class — that is, did not answer questions or offer suggestions, and who usually remained silent. The things most liked about such quiet students included the perception that they observed the social rules of talk and tended not to be disruptive. However, respondents also noted that classmates who talked only a little tended not to participate in group discussions and seemed shy and introverted.

In terms of having talkative or quiet classmates as friends, respondents generally showed no preference for either type of student. However, if they had to choose between the two types, they were somewhat more likely to prefer a quiet person as a friend.

About one-third of the students did not feel comfortable when talking to the entire class. However, almost all students mentioned that they had no problems if they had to talk to a small group or to only one other student.

They elaborated on their sources of discomfort when talking to the whole class. Their reasons for feeling uncomfortable included feeling embarrassed, nervous, and afraid; worrying about how their classmates would react to them; fears of being ridiculed or criticized; and feeling shy.

There were some gender differences in terms of the sources of discomfort when talking to the whole class. Females were more concerned than males about the correct presentation of information and about the reactions of their classmates. Males expressed more concerns than females about being nervous or embarrassed.

Teachers' Perceptions of Children's Classroom Talk

Teachers in the four project schools were also surveyed. One section of the questionnaire dealt with the functions and uses of talk in the classroom. Teachers were also asked to express their concerns about the way students talk and about encouraging talk in their classrooms. Eighty-eight of the 109 teachers in the four schools completed the survey, a response rate of 81 percent.

The functions that talk served in their classrooms were grouped under a number of headings, such as work talk, social talk, emotional talk, etc. The teachers believed that talk served a useful function in the learning process since it was involved in such domains as problem solving, questioning, inquiring, and explaining. Teachers also commented on the role of talk in the teaching process; its use in giving information, directions, instructions, and explanations was perceived as essential.

Teachers also perceived talk as serving an important role in student-to-student interactions. Social talk in the classroom was confined to such things as interacting with peers, playing, and developing friendships. According to these teachers, talk was useful in providing students with opportunities to explain their emotions and feelings and to discuss issues of a personal nature.

The teachers also indicated ways in which they applied talk in their classrooms; the 88 teachers generated 175 comments. The major ways in which teachers applied talk included show-and-tell, student presentations, class meetings, cooperative work, and encouraging or facilitating free and spontaneous talk.

These teachers did express some concerns about encouraging talk in the classroom. Their concerns included keeping talk focused and on-topic; preventing a few students from dominating; and maintaining a high quality of talk. The teachers elaborated further on the quality of their students' classroom talk. They observed that student talk suffered from poor grammar, limited vocabulary, lack of clarity, poor structure, the use of street language, and too much trivial talk. With respect to the behavioral dimension, the teachers reported that some students did not listen to their classmates, and did not give others the opportunity to talk and participate in class discussions.

Discussion

The similarity between the response patterns of the two student cohorts is notable. Clearly, children form their ideas quite early about the people they prefer talking to about various topics, their likes and dislikes regarding quiet and talkative people, and what makes them uncomfortable when talking to other people. These early attitudes persist as children grow and develop.

Teachers realize the important role that talk plays in the teaching-learning process. However, they express some important concerns about encouraging talk in their classrooms and about the quality of their students' talk. One can argue that teaching "useful" and "meaningful" talk to children should be one of the important objectives of education, especially at the primary level. Teachers can develop situations in which children feel comfortable talking about their opinions and views, likes and dislikes, and expressing their feelings and emotions.

It is important that children learn early in childhood to communicate with others through the medium of talk. In addition, it is important that children be encouraged to recognize the importance of "useful" talk in expressing themselves. If this does not happen, as adults they may feel restricted when communicating with others. They may also lack the resources to verbalize their thoughts and feelings, and may have difficulty in maintaining a positive self-image when functioning in groups.

Conclusion

The writers of these articles have helped us shape a talk curriculum for our schools, and that curriculum, of course, cannot exist in a time-tabled session for speaking and learning in each grade. Rather, talk must be seen as a dynamic medium necessary for learning in all areas of schooling. Spoken language must be seen as a tool for actively engaging in a variety of activities that will increase not only the knowledge students need, but their ability to enquire, argue, reflect, and make sense of information, in what Jerome Bruner calls . . . "a forum — the aspects of a culture that gives us participants a role in constantly making and remaking the culture — an active role as participants." School must resemble a forum such as this, where children are permitted and encouraged to talk their way into learning, where exploration is valued, and where conversation is the most important mode of discourse.

We have come a long way since the days of silent schools, and now as educators we can begin to concentrate on strategies for making the most of classroom talk, not just encouraging talk production, but helping children to become aware of the content of the talk curriculum — using talk as a precursor to written work, involving oneself in a group task so that more can be accomplished, noting the effect of what is being said on the listener or audience, choosing both words and language style to suit the needs of the context, finding a personal voice that informs and connects to what others are saying using narrative as a means of sharing discoveries and hopes, working in role and discovering voices that were never even dreamt of, reflecting on the wholeness of every kind of talk in order to learn about self in relation to others, and appreciating the knowledge that talk is central to making sense in all learning situations.

The talk curriculum, then, is not a period in a day or a series of skills to be conquered; it is the result of a realization that schools can focus their energies on developing students who use talk to think, to communciate, to reflect, and, most of all, to belong. Perhaps Emily Dickinson says it best:

A word is dead   I say it just
When it is said,   Begins to live
Some say.   That day.

152

References

Kidwatching: Observing Children in the Classroom

Bruner, J.S. "The Role of Dialogue in Language Learning", in A. Sinclair, R.J. Jarvella, and W.J.M. Levelt (eds.), *The Child's Conception of Language*. Berlin: Springer-Verlag, 1978.

Halliday, M.A.K. "Three Aspects of Children's Language Development: Learning Language, Learning through Language, and Learning about Language", in Y. Goodman, M. Haussler, and D. Strickland (eds.), *Oral and Written Language Development Research: Impact on the Schools*. Urbana, Illinois: National Council of Teachers of English, 1982.

Piaget, J. *The Development of Thought: Equilibration of Cognitive Structures*. Translated by A. Rosin. New York: Viking, 1977.

Vygotsky, L.S. *Thought and Language*. Translated by E. Hanfmann and G. Vakar. Cambridge, Massachusetts: M.I.T. Press, 1962.

Talk about Text: Where Literacy Is Learned and Taught

Baker, C.D., and P. Freebody. *Children's First School Books*. Oxford: Blackwell, 1989.

Britton, J., T. Burgess, N. Martin, A. McLeod, and H. Rosen. *The Development of Writing Abilities*. London: Macmillan, 1975.

Bruner, J.S. *The Relevance of Education*. Harmondsworth: Penguin, 1972.

Chang, G.L., and G. Wells. "The Literate Potential of Collaborative Talk", in M. MacLure, T. Phillips, and A. Wilkinson (eds.), *Oracy Matters*. Milton Keynes, England: Open University Press, 1988.

Chang, G.L., and G. Wells (in press). "Concepts of Literacy and Their Consequences for Children's Potential as Learners", in S.P. Norris and L.M. Phillips (eds.), *Foundations of Literacy*

Policy in Canada. Calgary, Alberta: Detselig Enterprises Ltd., 1992.

Chang, G.L., and G. Wells (forthcoming). "Learning about Learning through Interaction", in E. Forman, N. Minick, and A. Stone (eds.), *Advances in Vygotskian Theory* (provisional title).

Connelly, E.M., and D.J. Clandinin. *Teachers as Curriculum Planners*. Toronto: OISE Press, 1988.

Duckworth, E. *"The Having of Wonderful Ideas" and Other Essays on Teaching and Learning*. New York: Teachers' College Press, 1987.

Durkin, D. "What Classroom Observations Reveal about Reading Comprehension" *Reading Research Quarterly*, 14:481-533, 1979.

Flower, L. "Interpretive Acts: Cognition and the Construction of Discourse". *Poetics*, 16: 109-130, 1987.

Fullan, M. *The Meaning of Educational Change*. New York: Teachers' College Press, 1982.

Goody, J. *The Domestication of the Savage Mind*. Cambridge: Cambridge University Press, 1977.

Heap, J.L. "Discourse in the Production of Classroom Knowledge: Reading Lessons". *Curriculum Inquiry*, 15 (3):245-279, 1985.

Heath, S.B. "Sociocultural Contexts of Language Development" in *Beyond Language: Social and Cultural Factors in Schooling Language Minority Students*. Los Angeles: Evaluation, Dissemination and Assessment Center, California State University, Los Angeles, 1986.

Lampert, M. "Choosing and Using Mathematical Tools in Classroom Discourse", in J. Brophy (ed.), *Advances in Research on Teaching, Vol. 1*. Greenwich, CT: JAI Press Inc., 1989.

Luke, A., S. de Castell, and C. Luke. "Beyond Criticism: The Authority of the School Text". *Curriculum Inquiry*, 13: 111-127, 1983.

Maher, A. "An Inquiry into Reader Response". Toronto: OISE, Department of Curriculum, 1989.

Morrison, K. "Stabilizing the Text: The Institutionalization of Knowledge in Historical and Philosophic Forms of Argument". *Canadian Journal of Sociology*, 12 (3): 242-274, 1987.

Murray, D.M. *Learning by Teaching: Selected Articles on Writing and Teaching*. Upper Montclair, NJ: Boynton/Cook, 1982.

Olson, D.R. "From Utterance to Text: The Bias of Language in Speech and Writing". *Harvard Educational Review*, 47: 257-281, 1977.

Olson, D.R. "On the Language and Authority of Textbooks". *Journal of Communication*, 30: 186-196, 1980.

Ong, W. *Orality and Literacy*. New York: Methuen, 1982.

Rogoff, B. (in press). *Apprenticeship in Thinking: Cognitive Development in Social Context*. New York: Oxford University Press.

Rogoff, B., C. Mosier, J. Mistry, and A. Goncu (forthcoming). "Toddlers' Guided Participation in Cultural Activity". To appear in J. Wertsch (ed.), *Cultural Dynamics*.

Rosenblatt, L. *Writing and Reading: The Transactional Theory*. Center for the Study of Writing, Technical Report No. 13. University of California at Berkeley and Carnegie Mellon University, 1988.

Scardamalia, M., and C. Bereiter. "Development of Dialectical Processes in Composition", in D.R. Olson, N. Torrance, and A. Hildyard (eds.), *Literacy, Language and Learning*. Cambridge: Cambridge University Press, 1985.

Schoenfeld, A.H. (in press). "Learning to Think Mathematically: Problem Solving, Metacognition, and Sense-making in Mathematics", in D. Grouws (ed.), *Handbook for Research on Mathematics Teaching and Learning*. New York: Macmillan.

Scribner, S., and M. Cole. *The Psychology of Literacy*. Cambridge, MA: Harvard University Press, 1981.

Smith, F. *Essays into Literacy*. Exeter, NH: Heinemann Educational Books, 1983.

Stock, B. *The Implications of Literacy*. Princeton: Princeton University Press, 1983.

Sulzby, E., and Teale, W.H. *Young Children's Storybook Reading: Longitudinal Study of Parent-Child Interaction and Children's Independent Functioning*. Final Report to the Spencer Foundation. Ann Arbor, MI: The University of Michigan, 1987.

Tharp, R., and R. Gallimore. *Rousing Minds to Life*. New York: Cambridge University Press, 1989.

Tizard, B., and M. Hughes. *Young Children Learning: Talking and Thinking at Home and at School*. London: Fontana, 1984.

Vygotsky, L.S. *Izbrannie Psikhologicheskie Issledovaniya* [Selected psychological research]. Moscow: Izdatel'stvo Akademii Pedagogicheskikh Nauk, 1956.

Vygotsky, L.S. *Mind in Society*. Cambridge, MA: Harvard University Press, 1978.

Wells, G. *Language, Learning and Education*. Windsor, Berks.: NFER-Nelson, 1985.

Wells, G. *The Meaning Makers: Children Learning Language and Using Language to Learn*. Portsmouth, NH: Heinemann Educational Books, 1986.

Wells, G. "Apprenticeship in Literacy". *Interchange*, 18 [1/2]: 109-123, 1987.

Wells, G., G.L. Chang, and A. Maher. "Creating Classroom Communities of Literate Thinkers", in S. Sharan (ed.), *Cooperative Learning: Theory and Research*. New York: Praeger, 1990.

Wertsch, J.V., and C.A. Stone. "The Concept of Internalization in Vygotsky's Account of the Genesis of Higher Mental Functions", in J.V. Wertsch (ed.), *Culture, Communication, and Cognition: Vygotskian Perspectives*. Cambridge: Cambridge University Press, 1985.

Our Own Words and the Words of Others

Barnes, D., et al. *Language, the Learner and the School*. Harmondsworth: Penguin, 1986.

Barnes, D. *From Communication to Curriculum*. New York: Penguin, 1976.

Barton, B., and D. Booth. *Stories in the Classroom*. Markham, Ont.: Pembroke, 1990.

Booth, D. *Drama Words*. Toronto: Language Study Centre, 1987.

Booth, D. "Imaginary Gardens with Real Toads", in *Theory into Practice*, Vol. XXIV, No. 3. Ohio State University, 1985.

Booth, D., and C. Lundy. *Improvisation: Learning through Drama*. New York: Holt, 1985.

Booth, D., and W. Moore. *Poems Please!* Markham, Ont.: Pembroke, 1988.

Bullock, A. (chairman). *A Language for Life*. London: HMSO, 1975.

Collins, H. "Drama and Language", in *Mask* 7 (1). Carleton, Australia: VADIE, 1983.

Halliday, M.A.K. *Exploration in the Functions of Language*. London: Edward Arnold, 1975.

Lundy, C., and D. Booth. *Interpretation: Working with Scripts*. New York: Holt, 1983.

Moffett, J., and B.J. Wagner. *Student-Centered Language Arts and Reading K-13*. Boston, MA: Houghton-Mifflin, 1983.

O'Neill, C., and A. Lambert. *Drama Structures*. London: Hutchinson, 1982.

Rosen, B. *And None of It Was Nonsense*. Richmond Hill, Ont.: Scholastic, 1986.

Seeley, A. "Classroom Research into Drama and Language", in *Dance/Drama*, 4 (1), 1984.

Smith, F. "The Uses of Language", in *Language Arts*, 54 (6). Urbana, Illinois: National Council of Teachers of English, 1977.

Stabler, T. *Drama in the Primary Schools*. London: Macmillan, 1978.

Tough, J. *The Development of Meaning*. London: Unwin, 1977.

Wagner, B.J. "Elevating the Written Word through the Spoken", in *Theory into Practice*, Vol. XXIV, No. 3. Ohio State University, 1985.

Wagner, B.J. "The Use of Role", in *Language Arts*, 55 (3). Urbana, Illinois: National Council of Teachers of English, 1978.

Wells, G. *The Meaning Makers*. Portsmouth, NH: Heinemann, 1986.

Yolen, J. *Children of the Wolf*. New York: Viking, 1984.

Learning to Teach by Uncovering Our Assumptions

Argyris, C. *Increasing Leadership Effectiveness*. New York: Wiley & Sons, 1976.

Barnes, D. *From Communication to Curriculum*. Harmondsworth: Penguin, 1976.

Bissex, G. "On Becoming Teacher Experts: What's a Teacher-Researcher?" in *Language Arts*, 63 (1986): 482-484.

Cadegan, M.J. "I Can't Stand Writing All This Stuff Again", in *Language Arts*, 63 (1986): 533-534.

MacDonald, M. "Looking for Answers", in *Language Arts*, 63 (1986): 436-437.

McConaghy, J. "On Becoming Teacher Experts: Research as a Way of Knowing", in *Language Arts*, 63 (1986): 724-728,

Montessori, M. *The Discovery of the Child*. Adyar, Madras, India: Kalakshetra Publications, 1948.

Neilsen, A. "Critical Thinking and Reading: Empowering Learners to Think and Act", in J. Harste and R. Carey (eds.), *Critical Thinking*, NCTE Yearbook, in press.

Perl, S., and N. Wilson. *Through Teachers' Eyes*. Portsmouth, NH: Heinemann, 1986.

Serebrin, W. "A Writer and an Author Collaborate", in *Language Arts*, 63 (1986): 281-283.

Settle, S. "Leading from Behind", in *Language Arts*, 63 (1986): 660-661.

Smith, F. "Demonstrations, Engagement and Sensitivity", in *Language Arts*, 58 (1981): 103-112.

Wells, G. *The Meaning Makers*. Portsmouth, NH: Heinemann, 1986.

Talking Sense: The Assessment of Talk

Brooks, G. *Speaking and Listening: An Assessment at Age 15*. Windsor: NFER-Nelson, 1987.

Brown, G., A. Anderson, R. Shillcock, and G. Yule. *Teaching Talk: Strategies for Production and Assessment*. Cambridge: Cambridge University Press, 1984.

Fox, J., and I. Pringle. "Screening Package. The Oral Language Portfolio. Draft Material for the Senior English Assessment Instrument Pool. Working Paper". Ottawa: Carleton University, Centre for Applied Language Studies, 1988.

Gorman, T.P., J. White, and G. Brooks. *Language Performance in Schools, 1982 Secondary Survey Report*. London: Department of Education and Science, 1984.

Halliday, M.A.K. "Language Structure and Language Function", in J. Lyons (ed.), *New Horizons in Linguistics*. Harmondsworth: Penguin, 1970.

MacLure, M., T. Phillips, and A.M. Wilkinson (eds.). *Oracy Matters*. Buckingham: Open University Press, 1987.

Pringle, I., and J. Fox. "Assessment of Oral English. Working Paper". Ottawa: Carleton University, Centre for Applied Language Studies, 1987.

Shea, J. "A Study of Gender Differences in the Language of Young Children Talking in the Classroom". Paper towards the degree of MA. Norwich: University of East Anglia, 1983.

Wilkinson, A.M. *Spoken English*. Educational Review, University of Birmingham, 1965.

Wilkinson, A.M., A. Davies, and D. Berrill. *Spoken English Illuminated*. Buckingham: Open University Press, 1990.

A companion volume to *The Talk Curriculum* is also available.

Classroom Talk

EDITED BY DAVID BOOTH AND CAROL THORNLEY-HALL

Speaking and Listening Activities from Classroom-based Teacher Research

A group of dedicated classroom teachers explore their experiences with talk. Based on a 3-year project involving almost 100 teachers, these papers by special educators include wonderful ideas, suggestions, and strategies for making listening and speaking an effective part of learning.

Classroom Talk features seventeen essays by teachers on various aspects of talk as well as ideas from many others who participated in this innovative project. The essays are grouped into five major areas:

- ☐ interactive learning as a classroom model
- ☐ relating text to talk
- ☐ talk as a way of learning in every subject area
- ☐ the role of talk in drama
- ☐ talk and the ESL child

Ideas cover topics as diverse as peer leaders in group discussion, talk and the quiet child, talk and peer conferencing, talk and computers, current events as a springboard for talk, communication through body talk, and much more.

This practical, hands-on reference tool will help teachers expand the effectiveness of talk in their classroom.

Proceeds from the sale of both books will go to The Peel TALK Project.